HARVARD ESSAYS

ON

CLASSICAL SUBJECTS

FIG. 1. The *Ara Pacis Augustae:* Restoration by M. E. Cannizzaro.
(*Bolletino d'Arte*, October, 1907.)

FIG. 2. The *Ara Pacis Augustae:* Part of the Processional Reliefs.
(Brunn-Bruckmann, *Denkmäler gr. und röm. Sculptur*, pl. 401.)

HARVARD ESSAYS
ON CLASSICAL SUBJECTS

EDITED BY

HERBERT WEIR SMYTH, Ph.D.
Eliot Professor of Greek Literature

Essay Index Reprint Series

BOOKS FOR LIBRARIES PRESS, INC.
FREEPORT, NEW YORK

First Published 1912
Reprinted 1968

PA
25
S6

1/63 Jensen 19.00

Q9839

LIBRARY OF CONGRESS CATALOG CARD NUMBER:
68-20335

PREFACE

SUCH unity as these Essays aim to secure is of necessity the larger unity of sympathetic interpretation of certain aspects of the life and thought of classical antiquity. Nor was a closer coherence desirable if the truest independence of the contributors was to be preserved. Two of the Essays touch at a common point, though but for a moment; and this coincidence was not to be avoided, as it is not to be deprecated, since asceticism with its passion to subdue the turbulent senses, is inevitably linked with the yearning after immortality which possessed some of the most earnest minds of the ancient world.

Regard for a more intimate association of parts might have made a book of essays on things Greek or on things Roman. But the less severe unity of the present volume is designed to bear witness, however inadequately, to the Harvard conviction that, for the purpose for which the ancient classics have their permanent and inalienable value, the literature and art of Greece and the literature and art of Rome are so intimately bound together that they may not suffer divorcement. We are all of us Greeks, we are all Romans. The Greeks are the creators of the one original literature of Europe. Roman literature takes over

and carries on Greek literature, tempers it with a moral impulse, endows it with an emotional quality; and withal has the consciousness that it is the voice of the nation that conquered and ruled the world. The Romans are the transmitters of the Hellenic ideal to the modern world; and their literature alone insures the continuity of ancient and modern culture.

The ancient world still speaks to the changing present, and with an undivided voice. The literature, the philosophy, and the art of the last four centuries have been fostered by the literature, philosophy, and art of Greece and Rome. An ineradicable influence that penetrates all modern societies, whose interdependence is marked by this common possession, is negligible only by those in whom the historical sense is enfeebled or absent. But, apart from this, and largely because of the very fact that our own modern world may be too much with us, it conduces to intellectual health to scrutinize ourselves and our works by the standard of an age, long over-past indeed, but an age whose aspirations are not alien to us and whose thought possesses an indefeasible power to clarify our own.

The contributors to this volume are all present members of the Department of the Classics at Harvard, with the exception of Professor Morgan, whose essay on "Some Aspects of an Ancient Roman City" is one of the last pieces of work he completed before his earnest and active life came to an end.

The Editor gladly acknowledges the assistance he has received from the friendly coöperation and generous support of many friends of classical letters and of Harvard, and in particular Messrs. Lane, Sexton, Ladd, Brandegee, Gray, Cummings, and Gardner, members of the Committee appointed by the Board of Overseers to visit the Department of the Classics.

HERBERT WEIR SMYTH.

CAMBRIDGE, September 1, 1911.

CONTENTS

I

THE NEW CRITICISM OF ROMAN ART

II

NOTIONS OF HUMANITY AMONG THE GREEKS

III

AN ANCIENT LETTER-WRITER — ALCIPHRON

IV

GREEK AND ROMAN ASCETIC TENDENCIES

V

SOME ASPECTS OF AN ANCIENT ROMAN CITY

I

THE NEW CRITICISM OF ROMAN ART

By GEORGE H. CHASE

THE NEW CRITICISM OF ROMAN ART

In the history of classical studies, one of the most curious chapters is that which concerns the study of Roman sculpture and the estimates of its importance and value at different periods since the Renaissance. To the exponents of that *scienza antiquaria*, out of which was gradually evolved the modern study of classical archaeology, the Roman statues and reliefs found in Italy seemed not only to represent the highest attainment of the sculptors of antiquity, but almost to exceed the possibilities of human achievement. Even the late Roman sarcophagi, of which considerable numbers were known as early as the thirteenth and fourteenth centuries, were eagerly studied and discussed, and the praises bestowed on the great monuments of Rome itself were extravagant in the extreme. This general admiration for the relics of Roman sculpture was shared by the artists of the Renaissance. Raphael and his pupils are said to have sketched the reliefs of the Column of Trajan not once, but many times, and imitation of Roman models can be seen in the work of many of the Renaissance sculptors and painters. Even the belief that back of these Roman works, and only dimly reflected by them, lay the more perfect creations of the Greeks, — a belief which gradually grew stronger and was definitely formulated by Winckelmann, — did nor materially detract from the admiration excited by the Roman works; as late as the beginning of the last century, Roman statues and reliefs were eagerly sought by collectors and constantly studied and admired by writers on ancient art. In the eighteenth century, especially, no man, or at least no Englishman, who made the grand tour and visited Rome felt that he had fully improved his opportunity unless he brought with him on his return some relic of Roman sculpture, largely restored perhaps and more than half modern, but nevertheless an example of that "classic" art, which was regarded as the visible embodiment of all that was best in ancient life and thought.

With the earlier years of the nineteenth century, we mark a change. The removal of the Elgin marbles to England and the purchase of the sculptures from Aegina by Ludwig of Bavaria, above all, the opening of Greece to travel and exploration as a result of the Greek War of Independence, revealed to the Western world the glory of Greek sculpture at its best, in works unmarred by the modifications of the copyist and uncorrupted by the restorer. The result was precisely what was to be expected. Here at last men felt that they had come upon the source from which the artists of the Roman period drew their inspiration, that here, and here only, were to be found the supreme manifestations of the ancient spirit, beside which the products of the

Roman age could occupy only a subordinate and unimportant position. During the nineteenth century, therefore, most students and critics of ancient art devoted themselves almost exclusively to the Greek development, and the Roman monuments were more and more left to the historian and the antiquary. It is a significant fact that in the nineteenth century, though many large and elaborate histories of Greek sculpture were written, not a single book devoted to Roman sculpture appeared. The histories of Greek sculpture usually contain a concluding chapter on Roman art, in which the productions of the Roman period are summarily discussed, but the discussion usually consists of little more than disparaging comparisons.

Towards the end of the last century, however, we find traces of a new, and in some ways a saner view of Roman sculpture and of Roman art in general. In 1893, Riegl published his famous *Stilfragen*, in which he advanced the opinion that development can be traced in the imperial art of Rome, "and that, too, in an ascending line, not simply a decline, as is most commonly held." Two years later, Professor Wickhoff, in publishing a series of miniatures from a Vienna manuscript of the Book of Genesis, took occasion in his preface to call attention to some neglected aspects of Roman art, especially to certain methods of representation, in which, he also argued, the products of the Roman time mark an advance over all that preceded them.

Wickhoff laid especial emphasis on what he called "illusionism," that is, the treatment of wall-paintings and reliefs in such a way as to suggest depth as well as height and width, thus producing the illusion of actuality, and on the "continuous method of narration," the use of a succession of scenes, without definite lines of demarcation, to suggest a succession of events. The preface to the *Wiener Genesis* attracted very general attention, especially after it was translated into English by Mrs. Strong and attractively published, under the title *Roman Art*, in 1900. In the next year, Riegl returned to the attack, in his *Spätrömische Kunstindustrie*, and argued that, even in the neglected monuments of the third and fourth centuries, the sculptors of the Roman period made important innovations, particularly in the management of light and shade in relief work. And in 1907, Mrs. Strong, in her *Roman Sculpture from Augustus to Constantine*, undertook to discuss the whole development of Roman sculpture with special reference to the contentions of Wickhoff and Riegl.

In this attempt to "rehabilitate" Roman art, one fact is noticeable: the protagonists in the discussion were men who approached Roman art from a different point of view from that of most writers of the nineteenth century. Their interest was primarily in mediaeval and modern art, and their inquiries were directed toward determining what Rome contributed to the development of art as a whole, not simply what she borrowed from

FIG. 3. The *Ara Pacis Augustae:* The "Tellus" Relief.
(Schreiber, *Die hellenistischen Reliefbilder*, pl. 32.)

FIG. 4. The *Ara Pacis Augustae:* Sacrifice to the Penates.
(*Jahreshefte d. oest. arch. Instituts*, 1907, p. 187.)

Greece. Naturally their views have been vigorously opposed, and it is still too early to say just how much of the "new criticism" will stand the test of time. But the discussion has, at all events, called attention to a number of qualities in Roman art, and especially in Roman sculpture, which have not been sufficiently emphasized before, and has raised many new and interesting problems.

The monuments to which appeal is most insistently made by the new school of critics, to prove the originality and importance of Roman art, are the great historical reliefs, which are at once the best preserved and the most typical products of the Roman period, and their theories can best be expounded and criticised by considering four of the most conspicuous monuments, the Ara Pacis Augustae, the central reliefs on the Arch of Titus, the reliefs of the Column of Trajan, and certain of the reliefs on the Arch of Constantine. Each of these has its own claim to consideration, each illustrates one or more points in the new criticism of Roman art.

The Ara Pacis Augustae, voted by the Senate in honor of Augustus on his return from Spain and Gaul in 13 B.C., and dedicated early in the year 9, was one of the most splendid monuments of the ruler who boasted that he found a city of brick and left it of marble. It was erected in the Campus Martius, close to the Via Flaminia, on the site now occupied in part by the Palazzo Ottoboni-Fiano. At three different times,

beginning in the sixteenth century, workmen engaged in
enlarging or repairing the modern palace recovered very
considerable fragments of the structure, from which
the plan and elevation could be roughly determined,
and quite lately more careful exploration brought to
light several new fragments and cleared up a number
of doubtful points. The fragments are, unfortunately,
widely scattered, — in the Museo delle Terme, the
Villa Medici, the Vatican, in Florence, Paris, Vienna,
and England, — so that the decoration of the Ara
Pacis is almost as difficult to study in the originals as
that of the Parthenon. Several of the slabs have been
mutilated and restored, and owing to the fragmentary
condition of the marbles, there are several pieces whose
connection with the structure is in dispute. Nevertheless, enough remains to make the form and the general
arrangment of the decoration certain, and to afford
an idea of the style of the reliefs.

The altar itself stood in the centre of a paved square,
surrounded by a wall about twenty feet high. The outside measurements were about thirty-seven by thirty-
four feet, and all the visible parts were apparently of
marble. The wall was solid on the north and south sides,
but there were openings on the east and west, possibly
two doors, possibly a door at the west and a large window at the east. Both inside and out, the wall was
broken by pilasters at the corners and about the door-
ways, and decorated in two bands divided by a moulding.

The inner ornamentation was simple. The lower part of the wall was carved in plain panels (perhaps in imitation of a primitive enclosure of boards), the upper part was decorated with heavy garlands of fruit and flowers, attached by broad ribbons to bucrania, with a ritual saucer, or patera, carved above the centre of each garland. The decoration of the outer surface was more elaborate. The pilasters and the lower parts of the wall were decorated with vigorous floral scrolls, based on the acanthus, but enlivened with flowers and with figures of birds and other animals. In the upper portions, on the north and south sides, were carved two long processions moving toward the western end, and about the openings at the east and west were smaller reliefs, one of which represents Tellus, Mother Earth, another a sacrifice to the Penates. The subjects of the other two panels and the exact arrangement of all four are uncertain and of no importance for our present purpose. But the three sorts of reliefs, the processional friezes, the panels with Tellus and the sacrifice, and the floral patterns (including the garlands), are important, since each, according to the new school, illustrates a prominent characteristic of Roman art.

The processional reliefs are the most Roman part of the decoration. In both friezes, the subject is the same, a procession of dignitaries, heavily draped in tunica and toga, marching solemnly in pairs and evidently prepared for some religious ceremony. Among them we can distinguish lictors with their fasces, priests wearing the cap with disc and apex, camilli with incense-box, pitcher, and sacrificial patera. One youthful figure shoulders the *sacena*, or ceremonial axe. Most of the figures wear wreaths of laurel, and several carry laurel branches in their hands. Several are characterized as senators by the ring which they wear on the fourth finger of the left hand. Towards the end of each group appear several figures of women and children. The interpretation which most readily suggests itself is that it is the procession at the foundation or the dedication of the Ara Pacis itself that the sculptor has tried to represent, and this impression is confirmed by the distinctly portrait-like character of the heads, so far as the original heads are preserved. Several critics, indeed, have attempted to identify the most prominent figures in the northern frieze, where the presence of the priests and a greater number of lictors suggests that the principal persons are grouped, as members of the imperial family and the officials of the year 13 or the year 9. The idea which inspires such an attempt is probably correct; it is probable that the northern frieze represents the head of the procession and contains the figures of the most important participants, but it must be admitted that the portraiture is not exact enough to enable us to recognize even Augustus himself with certainty. It is generally agreed, however, that the two friezes represent parts of the same procession, and that the division into two parts was due to the exigencies of the space to be filled.

The subject is analogous to that of the Parthenon frieze, and challenges comparison with it; and such a comparison brings out several striking differences between Greek and Roman relief. The most obvious of these is the realism of the Roman work, which is in marked contrast to the idealism of the Greek. The Parthenon frieze represents the Panathenaic procession, but not as it actually appeared at any one time; it is the ideal of the procession, not the procession itself, that the sculptor has tried to place before us. This is evident not only in the heads and the bodily types of the participants, which the sculptor has obviously idealized, but in the dress, which only in a general way reproduces that of daily life, and falls in sweeping folds unattainable with any known material. Of the setting in which the procession moves there is scarcely a hint, hardly more than the marshals, who at intervals seem to urge on the laggards or check the speed of an overzealous charioteer. The figures move in an ideal atmosphere, far removed from actuality, just as in form they are more perfect than the actual participants in the Panathenaic celebration. How different is the Roman frieze! Here every detail that can help to convey the impression of reality is emphasized. The heads are carefully differentiated and suggest portraits, though we cannot surely identify the subjects. The dress is that of everyday life, represented in the heavy masses and confused cross-lines into which the Roman toga naturally fell. Details of dress, such as shoes and finger-rings, are carefully elaborated, and the sculptor even takes care to reproduce the reliefs upon the incense-boxes carried by the camilli. Several of the figures in the background seem to take no part in the procession and are doubtless to be interpreted as spectators, representatives of the crowd of onlookers through the midst of whom the procession moves. Everywhere the artist's endeavor seems to be to call up actuality, to represent the procession precisely as it appeared. In this contrast between idealism and realism we touch upon a fundamental difference between Greek and Roman art, which has often been commented upon. Wickhoff goes further still, and urges that the difference exists not merely between Greek and Roman art, but between the art of the East and the art of the West. Eastern art, he argues, — and in this category he would place the art of Greece, — tends always from the individual and particular to the general and ideal; Western art tends rather from the general and ideal to the particular and individual. To this general law there are admittedly exceptions, and it does not hold so strictly for Greek art after the time of Alexander as for the art of the "great period," the fifth and fourth centuries. But as a broad and general distinction it holds true, and serves to emphasize what is perhaps the most striking quality in Roman art throughout its whole development.

FIG. 6. The *Ara Pacis Augustae*: Detail of Garland. (Photograph, Moscioni.)

FIG. 5. The *Ara Pacis Augustae*: Acanthus Scrolls. (Photograph, Alinari.)

Another marked difference between the processional friezes and those of the Greek period appears in the management of the relief itself. The Greeks used both high and low relief, but rarely attempted to combine them. The sculptor of the Roman relief, in his desire to suggest reality, attempts to combine the two. Some figures are carved in comparatively high relief, others are hardly more than sketched on the background. In this we see the beginnings of that "illusionist" manner on which the new school of critics lay so much emphasis and of which so many examples are found in later reliefs. The shadows of the front row of figures fall on the figures of the back row, while these cast no shadow. Thus the illusion is created that their shadows fall on the earth, and the background seems to disappear behind them. The artist of the Ara Pacis has not gone very far in the direction of illusionism. His relief for the most part is in two planes only, though there are figures that are not exactly in one plane or the other and nowhere is a very high relief employed. Of such a treatment of relief there are sporadic instances in Greek monuments. The water-carrier who stoops to lift his water-jar on the north frieze of the Parthenon is in somewhat lower relief than the other figures, and in the grave-monuments, from the fourth century on, figures in the background are often not brought out to the front plane of the relief. But such figures are exceptional in Greek work, where the artist clearly preferred to work in a single plane.

The small panels from the ends of the Ara Pacis exemplify another marked tendency in Roman relief, — the attempt to suggest a setting by the introduction of elaborate backgrounds. In the Tellus relief, the background is simple. Tellus herself, a matronly figure, sits upon a rocky seat; her lap is filled with fruits and flowers, at her feet are an ox and a sheep. At either side of the goddess is a symbolic figure, — the genius of the water mounted on a sea-monster and the genius of the air mounted on a swan. Or are they rather the Aurae, the favoring breezes of land and sea whose kindly ministrations mean so much to growing crops? At all events, they are ministers of Mother Earth, like the *Jovis aurae* of the *Carmen Saeculare*, published only four years before the foundation of the Ara Pacis: —

> fertilis frugum pecorisque Tellus
> spicea donet Cererem corona;
> nutriant fetus et aquae salubres
> et Jovis aurae.

But the figures alone are not enough to convey the sculptor's meaning. Behind Tellus he carves growing poppies and ears of wheat, and below the swan at the left he suggests a swamp with growing reeds, in the midst of which a heron perches on an overturned amphora with water flowing from its mouth. Between the swan and Tellus a long stalk rises and spreads over the background. All these details are naturalistically treated.

The Sacrifice to the Penates shows a fuller development of the naturalistic background. In the centre is an
altar of natural stone, decked with a garland and heaped
with fruits, approached from the left by two camilli.
One leads a sow for the sacrifice, the other carries in his
right hand a pitcher and in his left a dish filled with
fruit and branches; apples, pineapples, and a branch of
laurel can easily be recognized. On the opposite side of
the altar stands a bearded man, his hair bound with a
laurel wreath, his robe drawn over his head, but draped
so as to leave the right side and breast bare. His right
arm is extended above the altar and in his right hand
(which is lost) he doubtless held a patera for pouring the
libation. Behind him a part of a second figure, leaning
on a knotted staff, is preserved. The interpretation of
these figures is not easy. The un-Roman arrangement
of the robe of the bearded figure, the partial nudity, and
the treatment of the head suggest that the types are
ideal, and the most plausible explanation is, perhaps,
that they represent the personified Senatus and Populus
Romanus.

But it is after all the treatment of the background
which is the most interesting part of the relief. Behind
the altar the sculptor has placed a slender oak, which
rises to the top of the slab, and above the second camil-
lus he has tried to suggest a rocky eminence, crowned by
the shrine of the Penates to whom the sacrifice is offered.
The shrine is worked out with the utmost care; the

blocks of the side walls are carefully marked, the Corinthian capitals of the corner pilasters are accurately copied, even the arrangement of the tiles on the roof and their antefixes are conscientiously reproduced, and through the open door, which occupies the full width of the building, the figures of the gods themselves are to be seen. The whole is worked out in the same spirit as the background of the Tellus relief, but with greater boldness.

This development of the background in relief was not a new tendency in Roman times. Its beginnings can be seen in the art of the Hellenistic age. In the reliefs of the fifth and fourth centuries, such as the Parthenon frieze, the balustrade of Athena Niké, and the decorative friezes of the Mausoleum, the figures, as we have already noted, are placed in a sort of ideal atmosphere and there is no attempt to suggest a background or setting. But in works of the Hellenistic period, such as the smaller frieze from the great altar at Pergamum, and in products of minor art, such as the famous Tazza Farnese in Naples, we have very evident attempts to suggest a background by the introduction of trees and flowers and stalks of grain, precisely in the manner of the Sacrifice to the Penates and the Tellus relief. Moreover, the so-called "pictorial" or "pastoral" reliefs, which probably go back to Hellenistic originals, exhibit the same fondness for elaborate backgrounds as a setting for mythological compositions or scenes from country life. No doubt many of these reliefs, as Wickhoff has pointed out, were carved in Roman times and so present analogies in style and workmanship, — in the management of light and shade, for instance, — to the Roman historical reliefs. But the fondness for country life and the attention to details which are so marked in this group of monuments surely reflect the spirit of the Hellenistic age, as it is reflected in literature in the poems of Theocritus. Wickhoff, indeed, regards the whole group as products of the Roman period, basing his argument principally on the Tellus relief. But there is some evidence to show that this itself was copied from an earlier, Hellenistic work, and the balance of evidence is still in favor of the older hypothesis, which regards the "pictorial" reliefs as based on Hellenistic originals and the development of the background in relief work as one which took place in the Hellenistic age. The device evidently appealed strongly to Roman taste. It is much used in later reliefs, in several of which the background is carved to represent, in summary fashion, the façades of temples and other buildings at Rome, — another evidence of that love of what is real and tangible which we have already noted in the processional friezes of the Ara Pacis.

The purely decorative portions of the Ara Pacis illustrate still a third tendency of Roman art, much vaunted by the new critics, — the great development of plant and floral ornament. On the Ara, two types of such ornament occur, on the outside acanthus scrolls on the lower parts of the wall and the pilasters, and inside, on the upper parts of the wall, elaborate garlands. Both these forms of decoration have prototypes in Greek ornament. The acanthus is a common decorative motive in Greek art from the fifth century on, most familiar, perhaps, in the Corinthian capital, but used also for many other purposes. The forms adopted by the Greeks are regularly conventional, following the recognized tendency of Greek ornament. In later examples, such as those that appear on the South Italian vases, there is an attempt to enliven the conventional form by the introduction of winged figures, human heads, birds, and other animals; but this development never goes very far, and the Greek acanthus scroll remains essentially simple throughout its whole development. On the Ara Pacis, on the other hand, the variety of the design is perhaps its most remarkable feature. The basis of the design is the conventional acanthus, springing in graceful scrolls from a central stalk. But the scrolls often end, not in the conventional palmettes which are regularly associated with the acanthus in Greek design, but in flowers of different sorts, conventionalized and made regular, to be sure, but so varied in arrangement as to produce something like the effect of a growing vine. This effect is enhanced by the small shoots and tendrils which twine about the larger stalks, and by the great swans with outspread wings that recur at regular intervals at the top of the design. Even more remarkable are the small animals which are introduced in the midst of the foliage, —

FIG. 7. The Arch of Titus.

FIG. 8. The Arch of Titus: Relief from Central Passageway.
(Brunn-Bruckmann, *Denkmäler gr. und röm. Sculptur*, pl. 497.)

lizards and scorpions, snakes and birds, — and, on the pilasters, more elaborate types, a bird feeding its young, an owl with a snake in its claws, an eagle which has seized a hare. In all this, we recognize again the realistic Roman spirit. The artist bases his decoration on Greek models, but goes further than his predecessors in the endeavor to suggest life, varying the conventional acanthus scroll with many sorts of figures drawn directly from nature, and trying in every way to suggest a growing vine.

Even more striking, perhaps, are the differences between the garlands of the Ara Pacis and their predecessors in Greek design. Garlands of fruit and flowers appear not infrequently in works of the Hellenistic age, especially for the decoration of altars. But such garlands are regularly simple in character, composed of few elements, and the component parts are rarely worked out in any detail. In the Roman period, the garland motive, like the acanthus scroll, was developed in the direction of greater complexity and variety. In the garlands of the Ara Pacis we find a truly marvellous range of fruits and flowers, faithfully imitated and skilfully combined. Apples, pears, plums, cherries, grapes, figs, pineapples, ears of wheat, olives, acorns, ivy-berries, poppy-heads, and sprays of laurel can all be distinguished in the heavy garlands with which the wall of the enclosure was adorned. Originally, no doubt, the effect was further enhanced by color, and the garlands must have resem-

bled very closely the splendid terra-cotta work of the
Della Robbias, which, even in their uncolored condition,
they strongly suggest. There is, of course, a direct connection between this type of Roman decoration and the
work of the Della Robbias; the later artists undoubtedly
drew their inspiration largely from Roman relief work,
especially from the reliefs on Roman sarcophagi. But
back of the historical connection lies a more fundamental reason for the similarity, in that each is an expression
of the "Western" attitude toward art, of the love for the
particular and individual, in contrast to the "Eastern"
fondness for the general and the ideal.

The Ara Pacis might well be called the corner-stone of
the new criticism of Roman sculpture, and in a broader
sense, of Roman art in general. In it we have a datable
monument by which we can estimate the strength of
Greek influence in Rome in the early years of the Empire, and the importance of the innovations which were
being made in accordance with Roman taste. It is evident that the whole basis of this art is Greek. Every feature of the decoration of the Ara Pacis has its prototype
in Greek monuments. It is highly probable that the artists were Greeks. What little we know of conditions in
Rome during the first century B.C. points in that direction. Yet in many ways, as I have tried to suggest,
there are differences between this sculpture and its prototypes, and these, it is fair to argue, are due to the public for whom the work was executed, and are to be traced

back ultimately to Roman feeling and Roman conceptions. In this sense, it is quite correct to speak of the
Ara Pacis and other monuments of the Empire as products of Roman art, though many of them probably are
not the work of Roman artists. The point is of importance because it is so often maintained that the monuments of the Empire represent, after all, only a later,
degenerate form of Greek art, because the artists were
in most cases Greeks. But surely the *Graeculus esuriens*
of the period of the Empire, if his character is at all
correctly drawn by Roman writers, would have done his
best to please his Roman patrons, in art, as in all else,
and the differences which we can see between the monuments of the Greek period and those of the Roman Empire must be due to the influence of Roman ideas, even
though the sculptors in many cases, or even in all cases,
were Greeks. Wickhoff, indeed, maintains that "it was
only when Roman amateurs gave up their exclusive pa-
tronage of Greek artists and began to give commissions
to people of their own race that a change of style could
take place." This, he believes, happened after the time
of Augustus, since the Greeks of the Augustan time
had failed to create a style which satisfied their Roman
patrons. But it may equally well be argued that the
post-Augustan monuments represent the work of Greek
artists who had been trained in Rome and had studied
more successfully the demands of Roman taste. In any
case, the important point is that the Imperial monu-

ments, whether made by Greek or by Roman workmen, were made to express Roman ideas, and so are properly regarded as Roman art.

Among the monuments of the first century after Christ the new criticism assigns the most prominent place to the Arch of Titus. This structure, erected to commemorate the capture of Jerusalem in 70 A.D. and dedicated, probably, in the year 81, is interesting from several points of view. It is the earliest and simplest of the many triumphal arches, and the earliest datable monument in which the composite capital is used. For the new critics, however, its principal importance lies in the fact that in the two panels which are placed at either side of the central passageway, we find the "illusionist" manner in its most complete expression. The panels represent two scenes from the triumphal procession which celebrated the capture of Jerusalem. In one we see the Emperor in his chariot, conducted by the goddess Roma and crowned by Victory. About the chariot are ranged lictors and citizens, and two ideal figures apparently represent the Senatus and the Populus Romanus. In the other panel is portrayed another part of the triumphal procession carrying the most important of the spoils from Jerusalem, the table of the show-bread, the trumpets, and the seven-branched candlestick. In the representation of these subjects there is a marked advance over the timid attempt at spatial effect which we noted in the processional friezes of the Ara Pacis. The relief, says Wickhoff, "exhibits a subtle variation of depth from the figures of the front plane to the flatly worked heads of the lowest layer on their vanishing background. The common statement that the artist worked in three planes is not quite accurate, because the swellings and sinkings of the surface are very subtle and depend on the variety of effect to be gained, but not on definite levels. All relation of the separate groups and figures to the architecture, such as is maintained in the Pergamene sculptures, is here ignored or, more exactly, purposely avoided. A frame is simply thrown open and through it we look at the march of the triumphal procession. We are to believe that the people are moving there before our eyes; we are no longer to be reminded of pictures; rather the plastic art tries to attain by its own methods the same effect as would a highly developed art of painting — the impression of complete illusion. Beauty of line, symmetry of parts, such as a conventional art demands, are no longer sought for. Everything is concentrated on the one aim of producing an impression of continuous motion. Air, light, and shade are all pressed into the service and must help to conjure up reality. The relief has 'Respirazion,' like the pictures of Velasquez. But as it is the real and not painted air that filters in between the figures, it follows that all the master's art is brought to bear on such a skilful arrangement of groups as, in spite of the compression, may allow air to pass between, above, and around the figures, thus helping to supplement the modelling even as the sunlight, which, when it breaks in, awakens these figures to magic life. To allow natural illumination to contribute to the perfecting of the artistic effect was one of the boldest innovations. On the success of this startling experiment depends the whole marvellous effect of this relief, unequalled except in the Spinning Girls in Madrid. The task which Egypt and the East had in olden times set themselves, of reproducing extracts from real life with all possible truth to nature by the simplest means, had been interrupted for a while by the noble drama of Hellenism, with its ideal representations of spiritual and physical powers; but now that the interlude was over, the old task was resumed and brought to satisfying completeness by the most refined methods of a style aiming at illusionism."

Few, perhaps, will be inclined to go as far as this in praise of these reliefs. Indeed, other critics, less enthusiastic than Wickhoff, have not been slow to point out defects, some of which the protagonist of the new school himself admitted. It is obvious, for instance, that the designer of the reliefs had no proper knowledge of perspective; the drawing of the horses in the relief representing the Emperor is incorrect, and their relation to the chariot is obscure; and, in the opposite relief, though the soldiers are evidently conceived as marching through the gateway at the right, they seem rather to be passing in front of it. There is also a certain inappropriateness

FIG. 9. The Column of Trajan.

FIG. 10. The Column of Trajan: Detail of the Decoration.
(Cichorius, *Die Reliefs der Trajanssäule*, pl. 83.)

in the suggestion of an open window, occupying practically the whole width of a pier which serves to support a heavy superstructure. Yet in spite of these obvious deficiencies, one is forced to admit Wickhoff's main contention, that the sculptors of the Roman age saw and attempted to realize possibilities in relief sculpture which the Greeks had not seen or had consciously rejected, and that it was along lines suggested by the reliefs of the Arch of Titus that the sculptors of the Renaissance advanced. It was the "illusionist" method, combined with a correct knowledge of perspective, that produced such masterpieces as the Ghiberti Gates in Florence.

In the Column of Trajan, erected early in the second century, we have another monument which, like the Arch of Titus, has gained a new importance through the criticism of Wickhoff and his followers. The principal decoration of the column consists of a band of sculptured relief in which are commemorated the events of the Emperor's two campaigns against the Dacians. The reliefs have long been recognized as important historical documents, interesting especially to students of ethnology and of Roman military antiquities. To Wickhoff belongs the credit of emphasizing the importance of the method by which these events are portrayed. This is, to use Wickhoff's own expression, "the continuous method of narration." In depicting the events of the two campaigns, the sculptor has simply given up all attempt at unity of time and place and has represented the progress of the army in a series of scenes which follow one another in quick succession, with no clearly marked divisions between the different episodes. Within the space of a few feet, we see the troops cross a river, engage the enemy, defeat him, and press on to the siege of a stronghold or the building of a camp. The same figures recur again and again, especially the figure of Trajan, who is represented more than ninety times. The result of this constant recurrence of the principal person, as Wickhoff well pointed out, is that in every scene we look first for the Emperor, and such unity as exists is a unity of idea. Such a method of representation is common in early and primitive art. It appears frequently in Egyptian and Assyrian reliefs and even occasionally in the work of the Greek painters and sculptors. A cylix in the British Museum is decorated with six of the exploits of Theseus placed side by side, and in the smaller sculptured frieze from the great altar at Pergamum, the history of the Mysian king, Telephus, was represented in a series of successive scenes. Such cases are rare and sporadic in Greek art, where, with very few exceptions, unity of time and place are strictly observed and within the frame of a single composition, only one event is depicted, but there are enough of them to show that the continuous method cannot be regarded as something absolutely new in the Imperial period, but rather as a reversion to an earlier practice. On the other hand, it must be admitted that in the Column of Trajan this

method was developed more completely and more logically than it had ever been before.

The importance and the value of the new development have been variously estimated. For Wickhoff it
marks the culminating point in the history of ancient
art. "With the establishment of this principle," he
declares, "the development of art, that had begun in
Egypt and passed through so many different phases
among the peoples of the Mediterranean basin, is completed and closed. An incessantly active imagination
had allied itself to the realistic tendencies of this Western
art, and out of the materials that deceptive illusionism
offered had created a new kind of narrative, the *continuous*. This was the bright, waving flower that grew
on the strong root of realism." By others the continuous
method is regarded as a step backwards, a proof, not of
the creative power of the artists of the Roman period, but
of the weakening of the best traditions of ancient art,
of which the conventional background adopted throughout this series of reliefs is but another evidence. To
quote a prominent English critic, it is "a revival of a
primitive manner, which the empire of Greek art had
almost civilized off the face of the earth." Between
these divergent points of view, there is room for many
shades of opinion, but in any case it cannot be denied
that the innovation was one that had a marked effect
on the later development of art. The continuous
method of narration is found on many Roman monu-

ments of the second and third centuries, notably on the sculptured sarcophagi, it was taken up by the early Christians for the representation of the stories embodied in Biblical tradition, and profoundly influenced the art of the Middle Ages. From the point of view of the history of art, it is undoubtedly the most important development of the Imperial period.

Finally, the Arch of Constantine, built by that Emperor to commemorate his victory over Maxentius in the year 312, may serve to illustrate a principle which has been especially emphasized by Riegl. Of the elaborate sculptured decoration of this monument, by far the larger part was taken from earlier buildings. Only a few of the reliefs are contemporary with the arch, and some of these were probably carved originally for a monument erected by Diocletian a few years before the accession of Constantine, — a sad commentary on the decline of the sculptor's art in the fourth century. Yet even here, if we follow Riegl, evidences of originality are not entirely lacking. The most important of the "contemporary" reliefs are the narrow friezes which are placed just below the large medallions on the sides and the ends of the monument. They represent the battle and siege of Verona, the battle of the Milvian Bridge, the Emperor and his staff upon the Rostra, a *congiarium*, or distribution of gifts, and two scenes from a triumphal procession. In them all, the most striking feature is the tendency to isolate the separate figures and groups, and by deep undercutting to outline each with heavy shadow. It is not a question of working in many planes, as in the reliefs on the Arch of Titus. All the figures are brought out to the front face of the relief, but so framed in shadow that they seem to stand freely in space, and the background, in several instances, practically disappears. The tendency is not a new one in the fourth century, for its beginnings can be seen in sarcophagi as early as the time of Hadrian. But the age of Constantine marks its fullest development. In the narrow friezes on the arch the principle is carried to its logical conclusion, and truthful representation is sacrificed to decorative effect. Separated by deep shadows, the individual figures and groups, even in the fighting scenes, appear stiff and formal, more like puppets moved by strings than like living human beings. This suggestion is strengthened by the summary and unskilful rendering of the figures themselves, with their squat and heavy forms, and by the tendency to return to the "frontal" position which characterizes early and primitive art. But these details are of secondary importance. The stiffness and formality are due primarily, to quote Riegl's own words, to "the positive artistic intention clearly to differentiate figures and parts of figures from one another, while calling forth at the same time the optic impression of a rhythmical alternation of light and shade."

That this method of obtaining an effect of light-on-dark design by heavy undercutting is a new development in the Imperial period must be conceded. It differs both from the frank recognition of the background in Greek reliefs of the great age and from the illusionist methods of Flavian sculpture. That it is an important development is evident from the great number of Christian sarcophagi and Christian and pagan ivories in which it is employed. Indeed, it is largely because of the constant use of deep undercutting and the consequent isolation of the figures in early Christian art that the narrow friezes of the Arch of Constantine have so often been characterized as mediaeval or Byzantine in character. The method, therefore, whatever be its intrinsic merits, cannot be denied an important influence on the later development.

Such are some of the merits which these recent critics see in the Roman monuments of the Empire. The innovations on which most of their arguments for the originality of Roman art are based are those which I have emphasized, — the illusionist manner, the development of the background, the elaboration of naturalistic plant and floral ornament, the continuous method of narration, and the production of novel optic effects by deep undercutting and isolation of the figure. Like all pleaders, they frequently overstate their case and try to prove too much, and they sometimes fall into the error of trying to emphasize the importance of Roman art by disparaging the earlier attainments of the Greeks. This is surely a mistake, for there can be no doubt that in the

somewhat restricted field in which they worked and with
the limitations which they voluntarily imposed upon
themselves, the artists of the Greek period produced
works never equalled in later times. The originality,
too, which the new critics see in Roman art, is not, I
think, so great as some of them maintain. For most of
the innovations which they praise so insistently, certain
prototypes, or at least certain suggestions can be found
in Greek monuments, especially in the monuments of
the Hellenistic age, and it is highly probable that as our
knowledge of Hellenistic art becomes clearer, especially
of the art which flourished in the great cities of the Eastern Greek world, an even closer relation between the
works of the Imperial age and those that preceded them
will be made evident. Granting all this, however, we
must admit that the critics of the new school have proved
their main contention, — that in the development of art
as a whole the Roman episode marks a distinct stage,
and that Roman art can no longer be treated merely as a
later and degenerate phase of the art of the Greeks. If
they had accomplished nothing else, they would deserve
our gratitude for calling attention to this neglected
aspect of that Roman civilization which so profoundly
influenced all later civilizations of the Western world.

II

NOTIONS OF HUMANITY AMONG THE GREEKS

By CHARLES BURTON GULICK

NOTIONS OF HUMANITY AMONG THE GREEKS

PAUSANIAS was one day wandering among the monuments of Athens, still standing in composite completeness in the second century after Christ, when he came upon an altar to Pity in the market-place. The sight of it caused him to stop and reflect that "this God, although his functions are of special interest to human beings amid the vicissitudes of fortune, receives honor from none of the Greek states except Athens." Kindliness toward men, he goes on to explain, is a national characteristic of the Athenians.

We need not lose ourselves in the narrow streets of Athens, or in the still narrower back alleys of German speculation, in trying to keep up with those interpreters of this passage who seek to locate the altar in some other quarter than that mentioned by Pausanias; and we need not take very seriously the sentimentality of Statius, who wrote of this same Athenian divinity, *lacrimis altaria sudant* — "its altars sweat tears." There can be no doubt that the altar was somewhere in the city, that it symbolized a spirit of humanity which distinguished the Athenians above their contemporaries, and that this spirit found conscious expression in public ritual.

How early does the conscious exercise of the spirit

show itself? In Homer, to be sure, we have many scenes where compassion is the ruling motive. The *Iliad* leaves us, near the end of its story, with the picture, fresh in mind, of the aged Priam winning back from the relenting Achilles the body of Hector; a scene singularly direct in its appeal to elementary emotions of pity, and constantly quoted by lovers of poetry for the ethical contrast it affords to the ferocity of Achilles revealed in the earlier part of the story. In the *Odyssey* we mark an advance, — "it is not holy to exult over slain foemen." Here a religious motive, marking the deeper responsibility of a whole community, makes clearer the irresponsibility of Achilles' position, so far as a feeling of duty is concerned. These two examples, thus slightly differing in kind, are witnesses to a milder feeling which was beginning to supersede the savage notions and ideals wherewith the earliest Ionic civilization must have been beset. They are of interest here only because they show the germ of what was later to become normal. A new ethical order is in conflict with the prejudices of the old, whereas by the fifth century the spiritual heirs of Ionia have come to recognize clemency and generosity as accepted ideals. Thus Pindar, idealizing the Lydian Croesus, benefactor of Delphi, as was the fashion in the early fifth century, says of him: "The kindliness of Croesus fadeth not away, whereas men tell everywhere with hate of him who burned men within a brazen bull, Phalaris of pitiless heart."

Against the inhuman and savage details of ancient myth the fifth century, as is well known, made effective revolt, which might take the form of aesthetic repugnance on the part of a poet, of indifference or temporizing on the part of the statesmen, of indignant protest from the philosopher. Pindar declines to accept the story that the blessed gods had ever eaten of the shoulder of Pelops, and, with more positive disgust, Euripides tells how the sun turned his face away rather than behold the cannibalism of the "Thyestean meal"; and Socrates denies outright the credibility of such stories of cruelty as that of the mutilation of Uranos by Kronos.

On the other hand, the reader of Herodotus cannot help fancying that he, true to his aim of glorifying Athens, is fond of holding up before his Athenian hearers, by way of complacent contrast, pictures of Oriental or Egyptian cruelty which will fascinate and horrify. The very refinement of cruelty is realized in characteristic Oriental fashion in the punishment meted out to one Sisamnes. He, Herodotus tells us, was a Persian judge whom Cambyses caused to be killed and flayed for a corrupt decision. His son Otanes was promoted to the judgment-seat, which was upholstered with his father's skin. The historian vouchsafes no moralizing comment, but it is plain that here, as also in his narrative of the cannibal atrocities of Astyages, the Mede, toward Harpagus, or of Psammetichus the Egyptian cutting out the tongues of women, that he is reproducing for the entertainment of his hearers what he believes to be the true and necessary conception of an inhuman Eastern monarch.

Of the contrast of all this with himself, at home and in Athens, the Greek had a thorough understanding. A poor old cripple, pleading before the Council for the continuance of his annual pension, says, in a speech written by Lysias: "Do not take away from me, who am growing older and feebler, what you gave to me when I was younger and stronger, especially when you have the reputation of being the most merciful people in the world." This, it may be said, is only the cajolery and flattery of a special pleader — the "Sweet Sir" or "Kind Sir" of all beggars. But it means more than that. Pausanias, whose corroborative words we read at the outset, had no ulterior reason for his dictum; he stands at an impartial distance of six centuries from the cripple. Nevertheless, it may be well to recall other traits of the Athenian character which are allied to pity, and which make the Athenians the most humane folk of the ancient world.

There was, then, first, an unusual tenderness toward children. It is true that the exposure of infants, especially girls, cannot be proved to have existed to a less degree in Athens than elsewhere in the ancient world. On the contrary, at certain periods of economic pressure, amid the heterogeneous and cosmopolitan elements of the Athenian population, infanticide may have been commoner there than elsewhere. And yet it is none the less true that there, for the first time, we begin to hear something of the problems and responsibilities of parenthood. The Athenians listened with sympathy to Euripides when he makes a character in the *Danaë* say: "Dear is yonder light of the sun, fair the unruffled surface of the sea, fair too the earth in spring-time blooming, and the teeming wealth of rivers . . . but no sight is so radiant and fair to see as little children in the house." They listened, too, as we should listen to-day, to Herodotus' story of how an oracle delivered to the oligarchical ruling class in Corinth had predicted destruction to their rule if the child of Aëtion lived to grow up. "So they sent ten of their own number to the quarter where Aëtion dwelt to kill the child, . . . and passing into the court of the house they asked to see it. The mother, knowing of course nothing of their errand, and thinking they were asking for the child out of friendliness to the father, brought it and placed it in the arms of one of them. Now it seems they had decided, while on their way, that the first man to receive it should dash it on the ground. But when she gave it to him, the baby happened, by divine providence, to smile up at him; and seeing this he was moved by pity to refrain from killing it, and in his compassion handed it to the next man, and he to the next. So it passed through all ten; the last gave it back to the mother, and they went out." The simple human quality of this narrative is as refreshing as anything which Herodotus, a singularly human writer, has left us. One cannot help remembering, by contrast, how the tender lyrics of the Hebrew psalm of captivity are marred by the closing words: "Happy shall he be that taketh and dasheth thy little ones against the stones."

From Euripides we might extract abundant evidence to show that the Greek in general and the Athenian in particular was a child-loving race. Indeed, outside the vase-paintings, I know of no better spokesman for the child than Euripides, "the human." To be sure, in one passage in the *Medea*, we have a somewhat tasteless expression of doubt as to the wisdom of having children — doubt born, of course, of the sophistic questioning of all the facts of life which was the tendency of the time. "They who have no children, who have not yet begot them because they could not tell whether children are a blessing or a curse, are free from many troubles; whereas I see those in whose houses the sweet bloom of childhood flowers wasted with many cares." But the passage is saved from banality by the anguish of a parent whose children are torn from him just as their true promise begins to reveal itself: "Here is the grief that comes to all mortals. Suppose the children have reached their maturity, and are good; if it so befall, there comes that power, Death, who snatches them up and is away with them to the underworld." Beside the pang felt at the transitoriness of all things human — that pang which causes the melancholy in all Greek expression from the

Homeric poems down to the last gleam of Hellenic genius
in the Anthology — we can mark here the outpouring of
a personal parental experience. We are told that among
the Persians a boy did not come into his father's presence, but lived only with the women, until he was five
years old, so that if he died, his death could cause his
father no grief. Herodotus cites the custom with approval. By the end of the fourth century a considerable
literature had grown up dealing with the death of children and the consolation which philosophy might bring
to the relief of the bereaved. From this literature the
Academician Crantor culled the best in behalf of a father
who had lost his children, compiling what Cicero calls a
"golden book that should be learned by heart."

Compassion toward the crippled was generally inspired by fear of Nemesis, the retribution that levels the
proud. Greeks seldom forgot her power. Demosthenes,
in a rebuke administered to his opponent Aeschines,
nobly says: "For myself, when one who is but human
reproaches another for his ill fortune, I can only regard
him as lacking sense. For though a man may think he is
prosperous, believing that he enjoys the best of fortune,
he cannot be sure that it will abide unchanged until the
evening. How then can he talk about it or reproach
others for his lack of it?" Of course the compassionate
attitude might be strained, and pity might be marred by
condescension. " 'T is better to be envied than be pit-
ied," said a Greek proverb. But in general the Greek,

ever mindful of the possible envy of the gods, felt that it was unsafe to exult over his neighbor's misfortune.

But though the thought of Nemesis, like any other self-interest, may have stood too near to the Greek in many a transaction, and her shadow may have darkened the natural lustre of a good deed toward a cripple, it could hardly have been Nemesis that tempered the Athenian masters' treatment of their slaves. Nothing but native kindliness explains the freedom generally accorded to a slave's coming and going, the toleration of his garrulity and frankness, which the Spartans, less gracious and graceful masters, observed with aversion in their northern neighbors. The Romans of an earlier time knew something of the free and intimate intercourse between master and slave which marked Athenian urban life; Cato worked and even ate with them. But the later Roman found, as the Spartan always had, this freedom irksome, and it is significant that we first read of a slave uprising in Attica under the Roman domination of the country.

In the conception of what we should call *humane*, the Greek would have included his four cardinal virtues, — wisdom, courage, justice, and self-control. These, at least, lay within the clear range of his ideals when summing up human virtue, and with them he would have put, as less virile, perhaps, but none the less essential, the virtues of urbanity, delicacy, modesty, resignation. The last is declared by Schopenhauer to constitute the essence of tragedy; and imagining that he cannot find it among the Greeks, he denies to them, in the field of dramatic art, the production of a perfect tragedy. Yet one need only recall Alcestis, patiently resigned to meet death that her impossible husband may live; or Macaria and Iphigenia, sacrificed to save their city and people; or the wandering Oedipus, blind and homeless in Attica, saying less in complaint than in sadness, "Little can I ask, and less than little do I get, yet am I content. For patience is the lesson I have learnt from suffering and the long years." Surely Greek literature, and Greek drama at its best, is fully alive to both the ethical and the theatrical qualities of resignation as a human motive. There is a curious story told of the orator Antiphon, that he retired from Athens to Corinth and devoted his art of persuasion to giving spiritual consolation to the distressed, like a physician who undertakes confidently to provide relief for physical ills. One of the functions of that late *humanitas*, with which we associate Cicero especially, was to afford consolation in trouble. It is not quite correct, as has so often been done, altogether to deny to the Greek even of the radiant fifth century, that spiritual stuff out of which are made the martyr, the hermit, and shall we add, with Antiphon in mind, the faith-healer. The Greek sense of humor, it is true, sometimes intervened in situations which the Christian Fathers would have regarded too serious to justify levity. The meekness of Socrates becomes his well-known irony.

But even this is called *humanitas* by Cicero, who surely ought to have known whether or not that was an appropriate term.

One need not seek far to find the humanitarian motive actively influencing Greek conduct. It would, of course, be absurd to deny that the Greek, with his tendency to overreaching, did not recognize the profit to be occasionally derived from a good action. He would have accepted the dictum of the Roman philosopher, *est enim non modo liberale paulum nonnunquam de suo iure decedere, sed interdum etiam fructuosum* — "Sometimes it is not only generous to renounce one's right, but actually profitable." One may even concede that the average commercial Greek might not even see his advantage here, but be eager to reap his immediate profit at all costs to his future character and customers. But it is clear that however sordid the motives were that controlled the daily market and official actions of the Athenian, he had to listen on festival days to precepts of ideal disinterestedness. "To help any man," says Sophocles, "with all the resources at one's command, is the noblest of labors." Menander's lost play on the miser, imitated *longo intervallo* by Plautus and Molière, inculcated the positive duty of rightly employing wealth for human service, and was not a merely negative picture of the comic aspects of hoarding. The lesson taught by the Greek has been quite obscured by the Roman and the Frenchman.

Regarding alms — a Greek word, by the way, in which compassion was originally connoted — it was a well-recognized axiom that kindness should extend beyond the mere dole handed to the beggar to be rid of his importunity. "If you give alms, but heap abuse on the receiver, you therewith sprinkle wormwood on Attic honey." It is a common mistake in these days, due, if not specifically to Lessing, at least to the general misprision of antiquity for which the eighteenth century is responsible, to assume that courtesy, in the sense in which we use the term, was not known or practised by the Greeks. It would, of course, be an anachronism to impute to the Greeks anything approaching the *galanterie* of the French courtier of the seventeenth century; that would be to read away the civilization of the intervening Middle Ages, with its elevation of womanhood, for example. And ancient Greek courtesy, in the small fraction of Hellenic literature that has come down to us, offers only a few examples of the conventional phrase which in English and other modern languages has sprung from court life, and which, in English at least, has led to the indiscriminate use of *you* in place of *thou*, whether we are talking to a child, a dog, a friend, or a servant. Conventionality — that which is agreed upon as proper in any given community — is of course a relative quantity. It is a truism that ideas of conventionality will differ with the community. As the Greek put it "Custom is King," and illustrated it by pointing to certain Indian

folk who felt no compunction about eating their old
men, but recoiled in horror at the thought of burning
their remains. It would have been just as discourteous
to an Athenian to address him abruptly by name, without prefixing "Thou" or its equivalent as it is to-day to
address a superior abruptly by "You" without adding
his name. The simpler "O King" of the Old Testament
and of Herodotus may convey more courtesy than
"Your Majesty," according to circumstances. But admitting that the language of the classical Greek was more
deficient in this regard than that of the Byzantine Greek,
it is possible to detect increasing instances of a quality
related to modern politeness from the end of the fifth
century. A speaker in Lysias requires of his opponent
courtesy in address on the plea of a common humanity.
And it is not so long afterward when "philanthropy in
words" becomes a common phrase. Even Socrates ad-
dressing the judges, uncompromising as he is in his bearing toward them, is nevertheless prompted to qualify his
defiance with the words, "Were it not too rude to say
so." Plato also bears witness to that courtesy, rare in
any day or clime, which listens with tolerance to the
mis-handling of one's own language by a foreigner.
The comic poets thoroughly understood the fun-making
possibilities in a foreigner talking broken Greek, and
even Plato's testimony is given not without irony. But
courtesy remains one of the most conspicuous of Plato's
qualities; and even before Plato, Euripides, the spirit

most endued with sympathy and sensibility of all fifth-
century writers, makes the defiant Hippolytus say, "Aye,
there is great charm in sweet address, and gain won with
little labor." Beyond, then, the exigencies of political
invective or personal hatred or comic purpose, we find
courtesy as an element of that *humanitas* which may
without distortion of the historical perspective be ascribed to such spirits as Socrates, Euripides, Plato, and
Demosthenes. Here we may notice the contrast between
the growing delicacy of the fourth-century and the
rough-shod sarcasm and scurrility of the fifth-century
comedians inherited from the Ionian satirists. Their as-
saults ranged from the harmless mockery of peculiari-
ties in pronunciation and diction levelled against the up-
start demagogue Hyperbolus, to the harmful denuncia-
tion of the originators of beneficent public policies. A
jest is often the expression of stupid conservatism; and
Socrates in *The Apology* is made to voice his sense of its
injustice, although he does not dwell on it with self-pity.

These outbreaks of comic license, reflecting popular
ignorance and suspicion, are comparable to the recru-
descence of savage atrocity, which occasionally marred
Athenian military policy in the fifth century. We recall
the cruel treatment of the inhabitants of Melos when
that island was taken after a long and embittering siege
in 416 B.C. The worst counsels of demagoguery here prevailed. On the other hand, we read with the same thrill
of emotion, which can be detected even in the impas-

sive Thucydides, who tells the story of the eager race of the triremes to deliver, before it is too late, the reprieve of the Mitylenaeans, who had been condemned *to the sword* by an earlier despatch; and we catch our breath in grateful relief when the trireme arrives in time. Such occasions as the Melian disgrace were happily rare in this period of widening humanity, and when a detachment of the Thracian allies of Athens, turned loose to shift for themselves, landed in a Boetian town and massacred the entire population, including the boys in school, the incident is described by Thucydides as the greatest calamity that could have befallen the city. It is a question whether, in the doubtful state of his text here, the historian does not mean by "the city" Athens itself, so horrifying was the effect on the people there and on their esteem abroad. Her opponents could not fail to hold her responsible. Such excesses, which have too frequent analogies in America even in time of peace, do not disprove, rather they emphasize, the existence of a humane consciousness which worked to the surface through their power.

Again we must insist that the Athenians were conscious of their preëminence in the humanitarian virtues. Whether we take the *Funeral Oration of Pericles*, pronounced at the end of the first year's campaign in the Peloponnesian War, as his own production or as the rhetorical exercise of the historian, the document remains, unimpeachable and convincing, as the creed of a thinking Athenian. "A spirit of reverence," it says, "pervades our public acts; we are kept from doing wrong by respect for the authorities and for the laws, having an especial regard for those which are ordained for the protection of the injured as well as to those unwritten laws which bring upon the transgressor the reprobation of public opinion." Nor does it matter, for our purpose, whether this is the utterance of realized fact. The Euboeans, the Samians, the Thebans, the Melians, all might have denied it; but the ideal was there.

These virtues, then, of compassion, clemency, and courtesy, which distinguish cultivated man from the savage, which, in fact, make the substance of civilization, are readily observed in the course of Greek and, more specifically, Athenian history in the fifth and fourth centuries before Christ — virtues which Cicero sums up in the word *humanitas*, and which are connoted in the English word *humane*. Other concepts included in its wide range are those of benevolence and generosity, affability, love of family and children, and devotion to friends; and since the perfect virtue to a Greek was that which made him a perfect citizen and member of society, he would include elegance, cheerfulness, wit, and tact. The attitude here implied is opposed alike to the austerity of officialdom and the rigidity of professional and technical aims and methods. Further, within the limits of the idea of the humane, as we trace its expression among the different figures of Athenian society, we may include the notions of leisure and leisurely reflection, culture and learning, appreciation of art and of the artistic and the beautiful everywhere, and the impulse to literary and artistic creation. Here "humanity" touches closely on the border of "humanism."

We are at once brought to the question whether the Greeks had any word which described this large conception. This has been denied by at least two German authorities of weight, who in their own writings have given abundant and tasteful evidence of the influence on them of Greek and Roman humanism — Schneidewin and Reitzenstein. The latter is undoubtedly right in regarding the conception of humanity, as we have reviewed it above, as of relatively late origin; but it is questionable whether it required, as he thinks, that the narrower ideals of the nations should be superseded by the larger conception of culture extending into extra-national, or, more specifically, Latin regions. The processes of true humanism, Reitzenstein believes, could work out only through the operation of two forces — the ancient culture of Greece moving in coöperation with, but also in a sense in opposition to, the newer elements provided by Rome. In order to make a humanist out of a Roman, perhaps this was true. But, because the *homo Romanus,* Cato's earlier ideal, needed to learn Greek in order to become a *homo humanus,* does it follow that the Greek must die and rise again in the later Roman, that he may show the qualities which make the humane man and the humanist? We have already examined the ethical ground, and we may add that the antithesis expressed in the words *humanus*, "merciful," and *ferus*, "cruel," (the same as *inhumanus*), finds early utterance in Sophocles, in the word *apanthropos*. For this the older English *ab-hominable* is an exact equivalent. In the next century we find Demosthenes using the word *anthropinoteron* ("more human" = "more humane") to describe the proper attitude of a man toward misfortune. This is quite in the spirit of a passage in Plautus, where we read that not to allude to a worried man's trouble is *humani ingeni*, "in keeping with a humane spirit." Perhaps the avoidance of the word *barbarus* by the Romans to express the notion of *inhumanus* was caused by the uncomfortable suspicion that they would not be excluded from that category themselves in the eyes of the Greeks. Of the two Greek words *barbaros* and *apanthropos*, they preferred for their purposes the translation of the latter. However that may be, *apanthropos* is the Greek expression for the narrow provincialism of the uncultivated. Plato uses it of one who isolates himself from the wisdom and judgment of his fellow men. It is surely a proof of the variety of the Greek vocabulary, not of the absence of the conception, that in the fifth century we come on another word, *monotropos*, to express this kind of isolation.

Was there, now, a corresponding word in the field of intellect? Before we answer the question directly, a brief

historical retrospect will make clearer the evolution of
the humane consciousness.

The Persian wars, begun under the leadership of
Sparta, but carried through to victorious completion
with the youthful energy and intelligence of Athens as
the real motive force, issued finally in an exalted feeling
of nationalism, in the first clear consciousness of antithesis to the non-Hellenic world. Athens felt herself to be
invincible; the democracy set itself to the winning of new
worlds, political, commercial, intellectual. In politics
this led to her fall; but meantime her commerce and
trade, her language and literature, had accomplished a
greater victory. Hellas had now a new standard in
Athens. Attic speech and Attic letters had become Pan-
hellenic. This is the significance of the fourth century.
With all its incompetence in political and military movements, this period of Greek experience was the period of
readjustment, whereby the essential predominance of
Athens in all that was vital for succeeding generations
was confirmed. Her culture lost its local and provincial
character, and armed with it, the forces of Alexander
conquered the world.

Only to a limited extent, of course, could even the best-
informed Greeks appreciate the meaning of the times.
Socrates had little notion of the splendid awakening of
which the Sophists, whom he contemned, were the rigorous agents, and of which he himself, with all his ironical
self-depreciation, was the prophet. Much less could

Aristophanes, with that slowness to perceive what the future had in store which seems to be the peculiar defect of the comedian, — witness Molière, — measure the importance of the new forces and ideas which he set himself to oppose.

Before it can arrive at the point of view denoted in the term "humane," a nation must first have won for itself its own esteem, as Athens did in the fifth century, as Rome did in the first. It must then see those elements on which her own greatness and pride are based absorbed by other communities, which in their turn react upon it. This happened to Athens in the fourth century. We then discover the consciousness of the first stage, when we hear Socrates saying to a heedless man, "Can you be *an Athenian*, a citizen of *the greatest city in the world in point of culture and power*, and yet feel no shame in caring for money more than for wisdom?" The germ of this we find already in Pericles' speech: "Because of the greatness of our city the fruits of the whole world flow in upon us, so that we enjoy the goods of other countries as freely as our own." This is on the material side. Again, "We are lovers of the beautiful, yet simple in our tastes, and we cultivate the mind without loss of manly vigor. . . . Athens is the school of Hellas." Almost in this very year a chorus of Euripides had been singing in this strain: "Blessed of old are the sons of Erechtheus . . . who feed upon the glories of art, moving luminously through brightest air, where once, they say, golden-

haired Harmony brought forth the nine chaste muses of
Pieria." Even Aristophanes, whose obtuseness in some
matters pertaining to the great achievements of Athens
we have noted, was not altogether blind, and says of
Aeschylus, "He thought the rest of the world — outside
of Athens — the veriest rubbish when it came to judging
the genius of poets."

The next step in the progress of the idea of humanity
is taken when the qualities of culture are conceded to
others outside the narrower circle of fifth-century vision,
and when, especially after military and political humili-
ation, new standards of merit are sought and recognized.
Precisely this happened to the Athenian people after the
middle of the fourth century. Still convinced that there
is a great gulf fixed between him and other Hellenes —
so much so, in fact, that with the retirement of Athenian
power the opposite notion of Hellenistic power and
Hellenism inevitably arises — he nevertheless has come
through bitter but salutary lessons to the conception of
a world which now knows only two fundamental dis-
tinctions, those of culture and ignorance.

This being the evolution, it goes without saying that
there can be no idea of humanity in Homer. Likewise
the purely individual or local interests of the lyric poets
exclude them from the idea. Euripides, whose fine
insight into the whole range of human emotional and intellectual interests brings him closer than any other
fifth-century poet to the idea we are seeking, is not a

humanist, any more than a humanitarian necessarily is.
The tragic poets in general set before us, to be sure,
ideal human personalities as types, and are sometimes
moved to do this through speculations of widely human
range; but they are, nevertheless, too much engrossed
with the national spirit of the society in which they
lived and for which they wrote to emerge upon the larger
plane of a view which starts from the individual solely,
and embraces the whole denationalized world.

The fourth century writers discover to us more clearly
the germs of humanism, and we find it inspired chiefly by
the awakening and enlightening influences of which the
Sophistic movement is the outward expression. Socrates
is the first humanist when he says, "The fields and the
woods have nothing to teach me; I learn my lessons from
men."

Now the word which expresses all this, and which we
constantly find in the writers of the last century of
Athenian productivity, is the word which we translate
"culture" — *paideia*. There are earlier adjectives approaching the conception, as where Euripides says "not
unversed in the Muses" for "imbued with literature."
Even Cicero, "that mirror of all the humanities in the
ancient world," is anticipated by Plato in one expression
which is quoted by Schneidewin to prove his humanistic
bent — the phrase in the speech for the poet Archias,
hoc concursu hominum litteratissimorum, "this assembly
of cultivated men." For almost identical terms Socrates

in the *Apology* had appealed to his judges against the confusion of mind in his accuser Meletus.

In the fourth century *paideia* — Culture — is a catchword of the orators, especially Aeschines and Isocrates. It is frequent in Plato, and we meet its derivatives constantly in the fragments of the New Comedy. The kindly temperament is opposed to that of the man who is rough and uncultivated (*apaideutos*). Throughout Aeschines' speech against Timarchus *paideia* occurs in its double reference to moral and intellectual cultivation. In Aeschines, of course, it does not attain to the real notion of intellectualism which we get in Plato, and again in Cicero's *humanitas*. Euripides, too, had long before Aeschines associated forgiveness and wisdom. The old attendant of Hippolytus, fearful that his master's aversion to Aphrodite may bring down upon him the wrath of the goddess, prays her thus: "Cypris, queen! Forgive, if moved by the heedlessness of youth he utters words of foolishness. Seem not to hear him. Surely gods ought to be wiser than men." Here is clearly the intimation that the larger wisdom exercises greater clemency. *Sagesse oblige*. The notion may be earlier than Euripides, but nowhere, so far as the gods are concerned, is it so positively maintained. We are told that the tyrant Pittacus, on becoming reconciled to some of the leaders of faction in the island of Lesbos, including the poet Alcaeus, remarked that "forgiveness is better than vengeance." But the remark is attributed to him by a late writer who is notoriously untrustworthy, and expressed a sentiment hardly likely to have had much weight in early factional strife.

Some of the qualities of the "cultivated" man, as reflected in Plato and in Menander, may be here instanced. It is insisted, for example, that the humanely and liberally educated man differs entirely from the man who may be trained in the same curriculum, but for professional ends. Socrates' young friend, the ardent and ambitious Hippocrates, confesses his eagerness to hear the lectures of Protagoras. Socrates at once assumes that Hippocrates intends to become a professional sophist. "You must of course know," he says, "that what you get from Protagoras will be very different from what you learnt of ;your schoolmaster, your music-teacher, and your gymnasium instructor. Their instruction was not for any professional purpose, or given with the idea that you yourself would become a practising expert in the subjects taught, but for the general culture which befits a man of the free class (*eleutheros*, *liberalis*) — a gentleman's son."

But meantime, in non-philosophical circles, it would seem — certainly Plato is little concerned with it— there is emerging the idea of *man* as a category. "What a fine thing is man, when he *is* man!" says Menander. So in this comment on a mercenary soldier: "You are a soldier, not a man! You're fed like any beast to be sacrificed when your turn comes."

It was the Greek of the fifth century who all unconsciously had been working toward this idea. Out of native sympathies thoroughly human, out of his earlier (if
later it became hesitant) belief in the potency of human
reason, out of his abounding intellectual and spiritual
curiosity, he was evolving a new and effective idea of
mankind. The Greek of the Periclean age, if as yet he
remained literally "unsophisticated," would have re-
proved any act that violated his sense of right or dis-
turbed his notion of good taste, by saying, "You could
not have done that had you been a true Greek." When
Medea, to punish Jason for his desertion, has cast aside
her natural feelings as a mother, and stifling her own
cries has killed her children, Jason says to her: "No woman of Hellas could ever have brought herself to do this
deed." Here we have the older, elementary division of
the world into two irreconcilable parts — the antithesis
of Hellene and Barbarian with which Thucydides dates
the beginning of the national consciousness, and on
which Herodotus has based his work as a governing
principle in the interpretation of history. Provincial
this feeling may seem to be and no doubt is, especially
when it assumes the tone of arrogance. Agamemnon
says to the Trojan Teucer — evidently with the applause of the audience who heard the lines in the theatre — "Bring an interpreter to speak for you; the barbarian tongue I understand not." In this particular, in
the comparative indifference to foreign languages, the

ordinary Greek never progressed beyond the stage represented in Agamemnon's remark. Themistocles is perhaps the most conspicuous example of a Greek who set
himself the task of learning the language and customs
of a foreign people. Respect for a foreign tongue was in
the Greek concomitant only with a respect for the foreigner. This the two "intellectuals" of the fifth century, Pericles and Euripides, possessed to the practical
exclusion of their countrymen. Roman humanism could
advance further toward a more universal compass since
it prided itself on the possession *utriusque linguae* — of
Greek as well as of Latin. Atticus, Lucius Crassus, and
Catulus, we are told, spoke Greek like any Athenian,
and when Cicero wishes to place his own political duty
clearly before him, reflecting on its intricacies and un-
biassed by the vernacular catchwords of party feeling, he
does it in Greek — a trait admirably, if sarcastically,
caught by Shakspere in *Julius Caesar*.

To us of to-day, whose experience of course has carried us further even than Roman cosmopolitanism ever
dreamed, the Greek separation of himself and his race
from the rest of the world may appear narrow. We are
too apt to forget the superior gifts of the Greek when
measured with his contemporaries beyond the border;
we forget that to him, as was said of the Jew, were "en-
trusted the oracles of God," and that his own ideals of
life were preëminently original, authoritative, final,
to be referred to no external standard. A Greek of the

fifth century, then, would be entirely sincere and unassuming when he objected to any course of conduct because it was un-Greek. On the other hand, in the fourth century his position was modified. This modified position we are fast approaching in Euripides, whose posthumous play, the *Bacchae* — last and most puzzling utterance of his genius — is clear at least in this particular, that in its wide perspective all barriers between Greek and barbarian are broken down. By the fourth century, whose intellectualism owes so much to Euripides, the Greek could now say, "You would not have done that, had you been *human*." He has come to see dimly, if not to realize as vividly as the later Stoics, the futility of his national aspirations. This does not lead him to "apathy," the Stoic position, but to the notion of a common humanity of which Cicero first speaks in definite terms. The Greek has seen the great Emathian Conqueror crushing the last hopes of racial, or rather cantonal, ambition. Henceforth Greek life must move in new channels of social endeavor, and the Greek spirit of the past, so long as it survives, must project itself into the life of other nations.

Now, what assimilates the Greek idea of humanism to the Roman and the modern is, of course, the emphasis on man as the centre and the end of it all. We have seen that it is man, as opposed to animals or gods, from whom come the humane virtues of mercy, courtesy, forgiveness, and the like. That this is a necessary consequence or coördinate of culture — *paideia* — is constantly exemplified in fourth-century writers, and nowhere more plainly than in a fragment from a lost play of Apollodorus of Carystus, where a woman complains of the stupid cruelty of war in these words: "Surely the fate that governs our lives is a boor, knowing no culture, ignorant of good and evil alike, rolling us mortals about helter-skelter."

With the loss of national prestige the centre of interest and study shifted more definitely toward the individual; man as the proper study of mankind was increasingly recognized, after Socrates, by the expounders of his doctrine. Each of them might have said, with Rasselas, "my curiosity does not very strongly lead me to survey piles of stone, or mounds of earth; my business is with man." Socrates himself, we saw, was in accord with this, in expounding the relation of technical to "humanistic" aims to the young Hippocrates. The worth of the individual apart from his advantages of birth and fortune is now more cheerfully conceded, perhaps nowhere more remarkably than in Menander. "Speak not to me of my family. Those whose own natures have no individual worth to show take refuge in family and in the memorials of their sires, counting up how many generations of ancestors they had. Yet are they no better off, for who has'n't had ancestors? Whoever has a nature tending toward the good, though he be an Aethiopian, is well-born." Similar passages may easily be found in the writ-

ers of the New Comedy, exponents as they were of a less
rampant democracy than that of the fifth century, but
even more liberal in its theory of what a democratic con-
stituency embraces. It must not be forgotten that, as
Aristotle points out, there were numbers of persons who
questioned the right of that sacred institution of the
Periclean age, human slavery. Menander is in fact the
originator of the much-abused *nihil humani a me
alienum*. We are not concerned here with the sincerity
of such sentiments. It is enough for us that they were
commonly uttered, so that by Cicero's time, and amid a
thoroughly aristocratic environment, we find him writing
to Appius Claudius Pulcher in this curious way: *ullam
Appietatem aut Lentulitatem valere apud me plus quam
ornamenta virtutis existimas*, i.e., do you think that any
"Appiusness" or "Lentulity" can have more consideration in my eyes than the real worth of a man's personal
gifts?

It has been denied that Greek culture included an appreciation of art. The Greeks, it is said, lived in an atmosphere of art which they breathed as unconsciously
as the air. The comparison is apt; for that they did not
always breathe the Attic air unconsciously the choruses
of *Medea* and *Oedipus Coloneus* attest. The criticism of
art, to be sure, appears only in rudimentary form prior
to Aristotle. But the introduction of drawing into the
school curriculum of his day shows that already the sense
of the artistic environment surrounding the child had

been keenly alive, to be finally crystallized and embedded, as so many other things have been, in the pedagogical scheme. From this time on we have the connoisseur and collector, the explorer and archaeologist, or the enthusiast with a clamoring exegete at his heels, journeying into remote regions to see a statue by Praxiteles.

A certain amount of wealth, or its equivalent, leisure, is of course the Greek concomitant of *paideia*. A learned proletariat was happily not one of the economic paradoxes that puzzled antiquity. The cultivated man is the antithesis of the peasant — *agroikos* — and whereas in the closer association of the classes which distinguishes ancient from modern society there is little that can be called snobbery, one may still sense the gentle exclusiveness of the dictum, "evil communications corrupt good manners," which Paul borrowed from Menander, as he in turn had borrowed it from Euripides. This is the motive which leads the man of the fourth century away from the agora to the country-seat. The solitude of the fields, according to Menander, is the best teacher of virtue; the city crowds mean strife and envy; city luxury may dazzle, but cannot comfort for long. Xenophon illustrates this Petrarchan kind of humanism in a little tract too much neglected to-day, the *Oeconomicus*,. and in his own example of retiring to a large estate in Elis to entertain his friends and write his books. This is another sign of the growing emancipation from state and national ties, of incipient cosmopolitanism, which as yet, however, does not exclude patriotism or nostalgia. The old, fifth-century dread of living beyond the home border was not entirely overcome. Epicurus might strive to comfort the exile with the reflection that all men are citizens of the world. "Wherever I go, shall I not find a sky, a sun, a moon, and the stars?" But the exile still answers: "The moon of Athens is more beautiful than that of Corinth." Atticus, Quintus Cicero, Germanicus, and Marcus Cicero inherited this nostalgia by right of intellectual sympathy — the sentiment for locality provided that personality were linked with it. This is the source of Herodotus' fascination for the places he visited. It lies at the root of Euripides' studied searching after remote cult-localities, to reach, as in *Iphigenia*, new discoveries in personality, human and divine. This is why Thucydides, intent on men as the measure and means of universal force, is content to overlook the splendid works of art produced in the period he specially treats. And this, finally, is the reason why nature, mere nature apart from man, has a properly subordinate place in Greek art and literature.

In tracing the manifestations of the idea of the human and humane, it may seem as if too much stress had been laid on the moral virtues rather than the intellectual — as if philanthropy and humanism were one. On the contrary, an age or people given over to philanthropic virtues may be singularly deficient in humanistic achievement. But with the Greeks the spirit of the one is the manifestation of the tendency toward the other. In

Euripides we see the spirit and the ideal of intellectualism, coincident with a new conception of human kinship. In him we pass from philanthropy, in the Greek, not the modern sense, to anthropism, — an ugly but conveniently antithetic word, — to *humanitas* as it motived the studies and intellectual intercourse of the Scipionic circle and its successors in the Renaissance. Whatever elements of grace and beauty the Greek discovered in the world about him took their rise in man as such. The gods — human forms with only slightly larger scope — were the coadjutors of man in the scheme of things, not the originators of progress. The best that had been achieved in history was due to elements purely human, and humanity remains for the enlightened Greek the ideal and norm governing his attitude toward life.

III

AN ANCIENT LETTER–WRITER
ALCIPHRON

By CARL NEWELL JACKSON

AN ANCIENT LETTER-WRITER
ALCIPHRON

THE subject of this essay is a Greek author seldom read and of minor importance, whom the historians of Greek literature deem worthy of only passing notice, if they deign to mention him at all. His is not a commanding figure and the influence that he exerted on the subsequent course of literature is slight. Yet he is the foremost representative of a literary form, the imaginary letter, which like many others owed its origin and development to the Greek genius, and the eminence that he achieved won for him the tribute of imitation by men better known to us than himself.

Alciphron is to us but a name; beyond the name and the titles, Rhetor and Atticist, nothing is known of him. There is ascribed to him a collection of letters, one hundred and twenty-two in number, which profess to be written by representatives of four classes of Athenian society, fishermen, country-folk, parasites, and courtesans. But these Letters, being thoroughly objective in treatment, may be searched in vain for a record of his personal experiences and feelings. History furnishes us with no facts as to the precise period in which he lived and wrote. Tradition has no story, no scandal even, to connect with the man's name. Like Longus, the author of *Daphnis and Chloe*, the best of Greek romances, he is enveloped in mystery. It is a singular coincidence that these chief exponents of two allied literary forms, the Letter and the Romance, should have suffered a similar fate.

But if history and tradition are silent, the imagination may be allowed to draw the outlines of this shadowy figure. Rhetorician or sophist that he undoubtedly was, he must have passed through a career not unlike that of others of this class, concerning whose life and activity we are better informed. If not a native Greek, he may have been born, like a Dio Chrysostom or a Lucian, in one of the cities of Asia Minor or in more distant Syria, perhaps in the third century of our era. In the silver age of the Greek world, philosophy and literature flourished more luxuriantly in the outlying lands than in Greece itself. It has even been conjectured from indications in his Letters, which however are very slight, that his nationality was Syrian. But wherever his birthplace may have been, whether he was Greek or barbarian, Jew or Gentile, after he had received his primary education and had reached the threshold of young manhood, his steps would naturally turn to Athens, the intellectual centre of the Hellenistic world. Her philosophical schools were thronged with students of all ages and nationalities, drawn thither by the fame of some great rhetorician or philosopher, and by the desire to complete their education. In these schools of rhetoric the effort of teacher and pupil alike was devoted to the purely formal side of literary study, to the acquisition of a style embellished with poetic diction and tricked out with rhetorical figures. Style for style's sake became the shibboleth of these schools of sophistry, and the models which the student was directed to follow were the classic authors of the fifth and fourth centuries before Christ.

This cult of style was a result of a revival of interest in the great literary works that Greece had produced. The historians and the orators in particular were regarded with veneration and were meticulously imitated. There was an earnest endeavor, as at the present time in modern Greece, to recall into active use Attic words, phrases, and idioms, and a school of purists, Atticists as they were called, arose who strove in their works to reproduce the charm and the grace of the literature of the golden age. Such ideals as these were held out to Alciphron, and in his Letters there is abundant evidence that he deserves the titles of Rhetor and Atticist, by which he was designated in antiquity.

Such at least was the nature of the education that others of Alciphron's class received. Later he may have become a professional teacher of rhetoric, wandering like many others from city to city up and down the highways of the Roman world, or he may have been established in a chair of rhetoric in some provincial town.

This sort of training is surely manifest in his Letters.

Indeed the prose letter itself is, we know, a product of the decadent art of these sophistic schools. It probably was evolved from certain exercises on which the pupil used his ingenuity in presenting or interpreting character in given situations. The characters as well as the incidents might be either fictitious or historical. Only a few names associated with this literary form need be mentioned. One comes down to us from an early period, that of Lesbonax, a rhetorician of Mitylene, who is said to have written letters of this sort in the first century before Christ. Two others, Philostratus and Aelian, were perhaps contemporaneous with Alciphron, and still two others, Aristaenetus and Theophylactus, were surely later.

Alciphron then can lay no claim to originality as the founder of a new literary form. In his use of the letter, however, he is preëminent. He employed both the types in vogue in the sophistic schools, the fictitious and the historical. One, picturing the life of his time amongst fishermen, country-folk, and the lower classes of the city, constitutes the bulk of his work. The other includes letters ascribed to well-known men and women who lived in Athens in the time of Epicurus and Menander.

Most of these Letters are, to be sure, artificial. There is insincerity of sentiment, conventionality, and oftentimes frigidity of manner. A fisherman proclaims his love in stilted language, calling himself a devotee of the god who bears the torch and the bow, and comparing

the object of his affections with the fairest of the
Nereids. Another, on being refused a favor by his
neighbor, writes a quibbling letter, which, though it is
an extreme example, is a case in point.

Encymon to Halictypus

I did not ask you for what you own, but for what you do
not own. Since you are not willing that another should own
what you do not own, own what you do not own.

A fisherman's daughter, when she describes her lover's
beauty, uses the labored and erudite manner affected
by the Alexandrian poets.

The Letters, then, lack those qualities of vision and
individuality that give distinction. This is not surprising when one considers that they were not actual letters
but the expression of a literary form, and that all literary types are apt to be in a measure artificial. In Alciphron's case, it must have been particularly difficult to
approach realism owing to the amount of rhetoric that
was expected to be expended on composition. Even in
private letters among the Greeks, such as are preserved
in the Egyptian papyri, there is oftentimes a note of
conventionality.

Another reason for this lack of genuine sentiment is
that Alciphron does not always draw from life itself, but
from a copy of life. His sketches of the daily life in the
middle and lower classes of Athenian society are apt to
be but pale reflections of the truth that others had ob-

served more or less directly, mere closet-studies inspired
by the perusal of the writers of the great period. Of
these none exerted a more powerful influence over him
than the comic poets, especially those of the New Comedy. So close is the relationship that exists between the
comedies and the letters of the parasites and courtesans
that the latter may be regarded as a continuation in
spirit of the Athenian comedy of manners. Some of these
letters are so flat and jejune that they seem like exhausted echoes. Many of the characters, as might be
surmised, are not vividly conceived and individualized;
they fail to impress the reader with a sense of reality
and reasonableness. There is a tendency on Alciphron's
part to look upon them as types rather than as individuals, to portray the salient traits rather than the idiosyn-
crasies. These fishermen, country-folk, and parasites
do not speak in character but in an idealized conversa-
tional manner, befitting a cultivated Athenian of the
better classes. They write in a certain uniform tone that
makes it impossible to distinguish the writer of one letter
from another by any marked individual characteristics.
Being devitalized creations of a rhetorician, doubly
removed from nature, and not creatures of flesh and
blood, they cannot feel the emotions which they try to
express. Indeed, it may be questioned whether Alciphron had an intimate knowledge of two of these classes
at least, namely, the fishermen and the rural folk. He
does not exhibit so accurate an understanding of rustic

life as Longus, nor does he describe the toilsome life of the fishermen with the same sympathy as is displayed by some of the epigrams in the Greek Anthology and the twenty-first idyl of Theocritus.

Again, there is noticeable an annoying disposition on Alciphron's part to allow his characters to moralize in and out of season. The use of banalities and shallow ethical reflections to point a moral or adorn a tale was strictly in keeping with the ideals of sophistic training. Compilations of proverbs and gnomic sayings were made to serve as store-houses for those who wished to decorate their compositions. Themes of ethical interest would be chosen and expanded and the suitable moral drawn, or, if the moral was given, a story would be constructed upon it. Thus in Alciphron there are many stories obviously invented with an eye to the moral. He rings the changes on such trite sentiments as the honest acquisition of riches, virtue being its own reward, friendships implying a community of goods, idleness breeding trouble, fortune being all powerful in human affairs, and hasty words causing mischief. He shows everywhere a fondness for moral precepts, gleaning them doubtless from such collections as have been mentioned and from other writers. As an illustration one of the fishermen's letters will suffice. The theme, seemingly a favorite of the sophists, for it was treated by Himerius in a later age, is that of a poor man accusing a rich man of having destroyed his happiness.

Naubates to Rhothius

You think you are the only rich man because you can entice my hands into your employ by the bait of better wages. This you can naturally do, for a cast of your net lately brought up some golden darics, relics of the sea-fight at Salamis, when a Persian vessel, I suppose, sank with her crew and stores, and when Themistocles, the son of Neocles, raised that great trophy over the Medes in the time of our ancestors. As for me, I am content to provide for my necessities by the daily labor of my hands. But if you are rich, use your riches justly. Let your wealth serve honor and virtue, not wickedness.

Excessive borrowing, whether of moral or of other themes, never makes for realism. And this habit is part and parcel of Alciphron's style. His Letters reveal an intimate acquaintance on his part with the poets and prose-writers from Homer to Lucian. The sentiment, with which the letter quoted above ends, is drawn from an oration of Isocrates. The description of the philosophers given in one of the countrymen's letters as "barefooted, pale-faced impostors" has its warrant in a line of Aristophanes' *Clouds*. A significant line from Aratus, "a single plank of wood wards off death," warns a fisherman of the dangers of the deep and induces him to seek safety by embracing the life of a farmer.

Alciphron's style is in fact a composite of heterogeneous elements. The pure Attic may be found side by side with the vulgar tongue. Words distinctly poetic are mingled with the prosaic. Current forms of speech, neologisms, and words of the Ionic dialect, — from all of

which, purist as he was, he aimed to keep his style free,—
creep in and assert themselves. The very manner of his
expression is also self-conscious. The evenly balanced
clauses, often provided with rhymed endings, the extravagant metaphors, the abnormal position of words
betray the art of the rhetorician.

In spite of such trite devices Alciphron nevertheless
was a real artist. His borrowings, whether of mere
words or more elaborate ideas, are woven closely into
the warp and woof of his own thought. When he describes a thief who had been caught pilfering a country-
house as "stern of looks, with arched eyebrows, possessing brawny shoulders and stout thighs," he has made
use of Homeric and Aristophanic expressions in the same
sentence. A rustic who moralizes on the certainty of
death and declares that it is impossible for a man to
escape this fate, "no matter how closely he shuts himself up in his room," repeats a sentiment that Demosthenes had used in his oration *On the Crown*. So deftly
does he select and combine that no incongruity results.

Within the limits of such art Alciphron shows no little
ability. Indeed, he often becomes a clear-sighted sympathetic observer of the manifold life that was displayed
about him, portraying in letters that assume the character of short essays in fiction the pleasures and the
miseries of the rich and the poor, and satirizing gently
the foibles of his age. He draws aside the curtain and
permits his reader to behold the varied scenes that were

being enacted daily in the houses, the streets, and the market-place of Athens. If a sordid side of life is presented for the most part, his Letters, though sometimes libertine, are never gross.

In these transcripts of life appear veracious types sketched with felicity and with rare power of observation. Here is the money-lender, "a shrivelled, frowning old fellow, holding in his hand old musty documents rotted by time and half-eaten by insects and moths," the vain-glorious soldier bragging of his exploits in foreign lands, the rich merchant from the Orient with an inexhaustible purse. Here is the gossiping barber standing by his shop-door, and the juggler with his three-shell game that mystifies the countryman. The physician is seen making his calls accompanied by his apprentices. Here are also tragic actors, comic poets, interpreters of dreams, tavern-keepers, and the philosophers of the various schools — all forming the pageant of life that moved through the streets of Athens.

We may look at one or two of these figures at closer range. Let us take first the philosophers. Academic, Stoic, Peripatetic, and Cynic, they are all uniformly described as long-bearded, barefooted, pale of face, solemn and austere. Outwardly they were the very presentment of virtue, but in their private life they were generally regarded as dissolute. Philosophy frequently served as a mask for vice, and the glaring discrepancy between the preaching of virtue and its practice is con-

stantly dwelt on in the Letters. Following a fashion set
in comedy and perhaps indulging his professional jeal-
ousy, Alciphron consistently holds them up to ridicule.
They all alike are visited with his satire, but one sect
in particular is the object of his thorough dislike. The
Cynics in Alciphron's time had gained a new lease of
life and the immoralities of which many of them were
guilty gave philosophy a bad name. Into his mention
of them he injects a bit of animus. At the banquet,
described in one of the parasites' letters, at which the
philosophers of the various schools were present, the
Cynic surpasses all in the indecency of his actions. In
another letter a countryman tells of the transformation,
the physical and moral degradation, wrought in his son
on his becoming a Cynic. In personal appearance the
youth is filthy and offensive: his hair is uncombed; his
old cloak leaves him half-naked; he is bare-footed, carries
a wallet and a staff of olive-wood in his hands. He has
lost his sense of shame, hates his old manner of life in the
country, and even disowns his parents. Some deity has
driven him mad.

In his description of these figures Alciphron reproduces only the striking traits that are obvious to the
eye, seldom going beneath the surface and interpreting
character. His method is essentially different from that
of Theophrastus, who likewise drew types of men in his
Moral Characters. Both found their originals to a great
extent in ordinary life, but Theophrastus sought the

weaknesses of human nature and the offences against good taste which would go to illustrate his definition of a foible. He gathers these manifold traits common to many individuals of various classes and combines them, producing a composite picture. Realistic as the constituent elements are, the figure bodied forth lacks unity and cohesion. Alciphron on the other hand attempts the portrait of a single individual, the representative of one class of society, selecting the characteristics common to members of this class. Though his figures conceived as a whole gain in vitality, they are not so plausible as some of the types of Theophrastus. They are not drawn with that particularity of treatment that is a mark of Theophrastus' style. Alciphron, in short, is not so keenly analytic and observant as his predecessor. The following letter is typical of his method.

I decided [writes a fisherman] to go to Chremes, the money-lender, and staking my boat as a pledge get four pieces of gold, that I might be able to mend my net. No sooner said than done. Chremes, that half-starved man, who knits his eyebrows and looks fiercely under them at you, relaxed his severity and gloom (he wanted my boat, I guess), raised his eyes, smiled at me a little, and said he was ready to help me in every way. It wasn't long after losing his sullen looks that he showed he did n't mean well by me. His kindness was only skin deep. For when the time was up, and he asked me for both principal and interest, without giving me an hour's grace, I saw he was the fellow who I knew used to sit at the Diomeian gate, with a crooked cane, Chremes of Phlya, everybody's enemy. When I saw into what a mess I had got, I ran home, and taking from my wife's neck the gold chain I had given her as an ornament in the days of my prosperity, made for Pasion the banker and sold it. And with the money I paid my debt, interest and all, and I swore, calling down destruction on myself, never to go near one of these city money-lenders, not even if I were to die of hunger first. It is better to die decently than to live a slave to an avaricious old miser.

Here is a type, but a type well-described. Broadly speaking, the types in Alciphron are grouped, as has been said, in four categories, fishermen, country-folk, parasites, and courtesans; though certain other figures, to be sure, enter into relation with these classes, as the philosophers and the money-lender just mentioned. We may consider together the first two classes, the fishermen and the country-folk.

These, it cannot be said, Alciphron was the first to create. They made their appearance in literature as types in the Attic comedy. In the *Acharnians* of Aristophanes, for example, Dicaeopolis, cooped up within the walls of Athens by reason of the Spartan blockade, expresses his hatred of the city and his longing for his country home. In a fragment of a lost play, the *Islands*, by the same author, the speaker narrates the joys incident to rural life, "to live in the country on a little farm, free from the worries of the city, to own a yoke of cattle, to hear the bleating of the sheep," and so on. Both Aristophanes and Menander wrote plays entitled the *Farmer*, and to Antiphanes and other poets of the Middle Comedy are ascribed dramas bearing the name of the *Rustic*. Furthermore, there are extant fragments of a play by Menander called the *Fisherman*. But how these poets treated such characters, it is impossible to discover because of the scantiness of the material preserved. In bucolic poetry Theocritus in his twenty-first idyl sets forth with sympathetic insight the laborious life of two aged fishermen, and Moschus in one of his idyls repeats a motive common to some of the epigrams in the Greek Anthology that to a fisherman earth is dearer than the gray sea. And in general it was a commonplace that the attractions offered by the country were superior to those of the city or the sea. Whatever Alciphron may have added to such preëxistent pictures, it is impossible to say. In any case we have in him the fullest treatment of these two types in extant Greek literature.

On the whole he presents his country-folk and fishermen as simple, unaffected beings, whom an isolated life kept ingenuous and unsophisticated. "I knew you," writes a farmer to his neighbor, "to be a simple man, a thoroughgoing farmer, smelling of raisins and breathing dust." Being conventionalized and idealized as well to a great extent, they lack the marks of boorishness that Theophrastus associates with rusticity. In letters that are simple, brief, and direct they tell of their experiences, their joys, and their sorrows. One fisherman describes the launching of the boats, the successful draught of fishes, and the profitable sale to the buyers. Another, unable to make his living on the sea, appeals to his

wife for advice as to whether he should follow the more
promising trade of piracy. A third shares his love-secret
with his friend. Still another reproaches his neighbor
for falling into the hands of a courtesan. The amorous
fisherman is a figure not appearing in Greek nor in Latin
comedy and may be original with Alciphron. A daughter writes to her mother protesting against marrying
her father's choice, and receives in return her mother's
unsympathetic answer that she had better obey or else
become food for fishes. Another writer asks his friend
for a disused net; another frightened by the proclamation of war resolves to avoid service by taking flight;
still another describes an outing held on his yacht by
a rich young man and his friends.

This same diversity of subject-matter is found in the
letters of the countrymen. Here is an invitation to a
family, which includes the dog, to come to a birthday
feast. Here is a plea for loan of corn in times of distress.
A father exhorts his son to desert the philosophers and
come back to the farm. A mother begs her son, who
hankers to become a soldier, to return and choose a life
of security. A daughter invites her mother to visit her
in the city and see the sights. A young peasant, who has
never seen the city, requests his more experienced friend
to act as guide. This desire that possesses a man to
change his environment for another is the theme of several letters. The fisherman tossed by the turbulent
waves longs for the peace and the security of the coun-

try. The estranging sea on the other hand tempts the
poverty-stricken farmer with the lure of riches in a
foreign land. The busy life of the city with its spectacles,
its festivals, and its pleasures, draws fisherman and
countryman alike from their dull, secluded existence on
shore and farm. The following letter gives the experience that befell a peasant in the city.

You remember I loaded my donkey with figs and cakes
and went to the city? Well, after I had sold them to an acquaintance of mine, I was taken to the theatre, given a good
seat, and enjoyed the sight of different shows. I can't remember all of them. I'm a poor hand at remembering and telling
such things. But one thing I saw made me almost speechless
and open my mouth in surprise. A man came forward and set
up a three-legged table, and placed on it three small dishes.
Under these he would hide three small, white, round pebbles
like those we find on the banks of rivers. Sometimes he would
hide them one by one under a different dish, and sometimes
all under one. I don't know how he did it. And then again
they would n't be under the dishes at all but would come out
in his mouth. Then he would swallow them, and gathering
the people who stood nearest him, he would pick a pebble
from his nose, and another from his ear, and a third from his
head. After that, he would make them disappear. He's a
knave, worse than even Eurybates of Oechalia, of whom we
hear so much. I hope such a creature as this never gets into
the country. No one could ever catch him; he would steal
everything I have on my farm and make off with it.

It is noticeable that in these letters of the fishermen
and the rural folk Alciphron chose to emphasize their
narrow circumstances, their hardships, and their sor-

rows. There is in fact an undercurrent of pessimism. Faith in the gods seems well-nigh dead. "It is vain to sacrifice to Zeus," writes a farmer plaintively, "he is with other peoples and does not care for us." Man is subject to Fate and Fortune. Nature is fickle and cruel and in her sterner moods portends disaster. Storms at sea mean destruction of men; on land, the inundation of fields and the ruin of crops. As sea and land constitute to fishermen and countrymen their main source of income, they look upon Nature as a hostile, intractable force, whose depredations are fearful and lamentable. They bewail the burning heat of the sun, the bitterness of the cold. The wolf devours the flock, the fox destroys the grapes. The harvest fails and hunger impends. The farmer in his despair is resolved to abjure the land for the sea. The fisherman wearied by unproductive labor looks with longing eyes on the security and the advantages of country-life. Family life is easily disrupted. The faithless husband who spends his substance on a foreign woman is entreated by the injured wife to forsake his evil ways. A fisherman warns his wife, who deserts him for the pleasures of the city, either to return home or to go her way. The son, the maintenance of the family, is easily enticed away from home by the wiles of a courtesan or by the preaching of a philosopher. There is then a note of complaint pervading these letters that sounds elegiac.

When we turn to the letters of the parasites, we find

Alciphron in a different mood. These letters are the
scherzo of his composition. In a series of vivacious
sketches, marked by severe realism, he presents the
seamy side of life in a cosmopolitan city. Against a drab
background move gamblers, parasites, rakes, paramours,
and prostitutes. Though the parasite has no exact
counterpart in modern civilization, he was a recognized
element in Athenian society. By his coarse jokes and
grotesque actions he played the part of a buffoon at the
banquets of the rich, receiving in return permission to
dine at table with his patron and the guests. In Lucian's
dialogue, the *Parasite*, one of this class defines his voca-
tion as "the art of eating and drinking, and of the talk
by which these may be secured," and its end as "getting
one's dinner at some one else's expense." Painfully
true to type are the parasites of Alciphron. They are
for the most part conceived in a spirit of boisterous
humor, and the scenes in which they appear resemble
in nature those of an uproarious farce. The picturesque
names with which Alciphron dubs them are quite in
keeping with this conception and bear witness to his
playful fancy. They are chosen with the purpose not
only of depicting characteristics peculiar to a class as
a whole, but also of bestowing on individuals the names
apposite to their character. So in this gallery of rogues
may be found, amongst others, Wine-lover, Run-to-
dinner, Ready-for-breakfast, Pot-licker, Table-lover,
and Self-invited. They are like their prototypes in the

New Comedy impudent and gluttonous, with no sense of shame, driven by hunger to endure humiliating experiences and revolting indignities. They are the butts for practical jokes of every kind; the abasement and confusion into which they are thrown contribute to the merriment of their patrons. It is this aspect of their life that their letters oftenest present. The following letter serves as an example.

Did you see what that cursed barber, the fellow who has a shop by the road-side, did to me? I mean that prating, garrulous fellow who has mirrors from Brindisi for sale, tames ravens, and plays a fine tune on his razors. When I went to him for a shave, he was glad to see me; he placed me on a high chair, tied a new cloth about my neck, and then very gently began shaving my beard, taking off the thick growth. But there he played the mischief with me. For without my knowing it, he shaved me only partially, and not all over, so that one side of my jaw was thick with hair, the other side quite clear. Ignorant of the man's villany, I went as usual without an invitation to Pasion's. When the guests saw me, they nearly died with laughter. All the time I did n't know what they were laughing at, until one of them, coming forward into the middle of the group, took hold of the hair that was left. I managed to root it out with a knife, though with great pain to myself, and now I 'm ready with a big club to smash the scoundrel's skull. For he 's had the impudence to play a trick such as even my patrons would not attempt. Yet he 's never given me a meal.

But these pleasantries may take a more violent turn. One parasite thanks his stars that he escapes a kettle of boiling-water which the merry feasters have in readiness

for him. Another's success at the gaming-table provokes
the disgruntled players to assault and rob him of his
gains. One more venturesome than usual, who has visited Sparta and Corinth, tells of unwonted experiences.
His rude hosts force him to swallow his wine red-hot,
throw at him as at the dogs the refuse from the table,
and strike him with whip and thongs.

The outrages which they endure form the burden of
their complaints. "I can't bear," writes one, "the blows
and the insults of these drunken feasters. The devil take
them . . . My face won't stand these repeated boxings,
and I'm in danger of losing one of my eyes because of
their blows." To escape this abuse, one resolves to go to
Piraeus, to earn his living by removing the cargoes of
ships to the warehouses; another, attracted by the
tranquillity of the country, turns farmer; another, on
being assured by a comic poet that he possesses talent,
is minded to go on the stage. In retaliation for his mis-
treatment, or to provide himself with money, the parasite has no scruples about stealing the food, or the linen
or the silver on the table, and brazenly admitting his
theft. When he is reduced to extremities, and hope is
gone, he meditates self-destruction. "So long as my body
was in the flower of youth," says one, "and able to endure harsh treatment, an insult might be borne; but
now that my hair is streaked with gray, and the re-
mainder of my life verges on old age, what remedy is
there for my ills?"

In general, towards his patron, the attitude of the parasite is marked by a spirit of loyalty. He apprises him of the gossip below stairs and of his wife's peccadillos, and he abets his master in the pursuit of his dishonest pleasures. To be repaid for his pains with kindness and material benefits is a fond hope that he ever cherishes; but his highest ambition is to come into the possession of means and maintain parasites himself, or else to be raised for his services from the status of parasite to that of friend. In this vein one writes to his friend.

If Therippides learns that this has been done successfully through our activity, we shall get many gold coins of the latest stamp, and rich clothes, and besides the right to enter his house without fear and enjoy its luxuries unhindered. Perhaps he will consider us not as parasites but as friends.

In the letters of the courtesans, the last class, Alciphron still pursues his characteristic method. He deals chiefly with types rather than individuals. That he is still under the spell of Attic comedy is very evident. His characters are drawn along the conventional lines. As a type the courtesans are the embodiment of avarice and venality. "They are," as the writer of one letter says, "in popular belief wicked and faithless, having an eye only to gain. They are ever at the service of him who has anything to give, and the cause of all evil to those who have dealings with them." Their greed constitutes a motive that is a commonplace in literature. Their shamelessness and infidelity are among their common traits. So Philumena writes to her lover Crito, "Why do you trouble yourself to write so much? I want fifty pieces of gold, and not your letters. If you love me, give me money. If you love money, do not bother me." So Petala writes to Simalion, "I want money, clothes, ornaments, and servants. Upon these depends the whole management of life. . . . Have you no plate in your house? Has your mother no money, your father no bonds that you can bring me."

This Attic type with its usual variations may be seen in several of the characters. Petala, as has been noticed, typifies avarice; she ruthlessly answers the protestations of her disconsolate and niggardly lover by brutal demands for money. The cynical Thais seeks revenge for the slight done her self-esteem by Euxippa, whom she had once befriended, and in another letter berates her lover Euthydemus for deserting her for the schools of philosophy. The jealous Leaena tries to abash her lover by scornfully disparaging his bride's beauty. The plaintive Myrrhina has recourse to witchcraft to win back her errant lover. The wicked Megara is an example of the class at its worst; intemperate and rapacious, she is endowed with no redeeming traits.

In some instances a similarity of theme may be traced between their letters and Lucian's *Dialogues of the Courtesans*. In the latter, Drosis is abandoned by her lover for the study of philosophy, just as Thais in Alciphron is deserted by Euthydemus. In Lucian, Musarium's calculating mother, urging her daughter to renounce her lover who has nothing but promises to give, is actuated by the same impulses that govern Alciphron's Petala. Melitta in Lucian, like Myrrhina in Alciphron, employs a witch in her efforts to retain her lover's affections. Such motives as these are so stereotyped that they can furnish no evidence of the dependence of one writer on another. Indeed Lucian as well as Alciphron is indebted to Comedy for many personal traits and certain situations, and both make independent use of their material. Of the two Lucian is the greater artist. The dialogue in his hands is endued with a spirit and a flexibility but rarely found in the Letters. The naturalness and the vivacity of the conversation are in marked contrast with the mannered style of Alciphron. In one respect, however, Alciphron's treatment is superior to that of Lucian. His Letters are for the most part free from the coarseness which disfigures some of the dialogues. For Lucian in a manner sometimes grossly realistic and offensive has dwelt on the sordid aspect of his subject. Hence in Alciphron the atmosphere is more wholesome, the lapses from good taste less grave.

Apart from these imaginary figures stand the *grandes amoureuses*, Phryne, Leontium, Lamia, Bacchis, and Glycera, historical personages, who lived in the latter part of the fourth century before Christ. With them are associated some of the foremost Athenians of the time, Praxiteles, Epicurus, Demetrius Poliorcetes, Hyperides, and

Menander. Their historic reality enables Alciphron to visualize them with greater clearness, and his reconstruction of their age adds a footnote at least to the history of Athenian society. These letters deal with well-known facts in history. Phryne praises Praxiteles for the skill with which he has modelled a statue of herself. The *cause celèbre*, in which this courtesan was involved, gives Bacchis occasion to send congratulatory letters to Hyperides for his successful defence and to Phryne for her acquittal. Leontium, annoyed by the unwelcome advances of Epicurus, which she sets forth at length, makes Lamia her confidante, and begs for the protection of her house. The letters are in essence psychological studies of the feminine mind, and though they bear traces of rhetoric, they have a naturalness, a lightness of touch, and a truth to nature that make them modern in spirit and sentiment. Lamia, Bacchis, and Glycera are the most attractive of all the characters that Alciphron has drawn. Into the analysis of their emotions he has put his best work. They are portrayed as beings capable of sincere passion, undivided affection, and delicate sentiments. Lamia's expression of her abiding love for the general Demetrius reveals her disinterested loyalty. Awed by the attentions of a man so powerful, she declares her own disbelief in her great happiness, and in the fulness of her love, admits her readiness to give up life itself to further his happiness. Bacchis is extolled by her rival Glycera for possessing a character nobler than her calling, and is mourned at her death by Meneclides as the best of women. To Glycera Menander writes in a lyric outburst:

What happiness can be mine without you? What can exalt me more than the possession of your love? Through the influence of your character and manners, my old age will ever wear the appearance of youth. May we then be young together, may we grow old together, yes, may we meet death together.

Glycera's reply to this letter, Alciphron's most pretentious effort, merits our attention. The occasion of her letter is the receipt of news from Menander that he had been invited by Ptolemy to reside at the Egyptian court. The letter presents a dramatic situation in which the conflict of emotions aroused in a woman's heart by the bestowal of high honors on the one she loves, and by the prospect of his leaving her forever, is skilfully indicated. The lively satisfaction that permeates her whole being moves her friends to ask —

"What great, good fortune has happened to you, dear Glycera, that you seem now so changed in soul and body and in every way? Your whole being seems aglow with joy and pleasure." "Oh," said I, in a voice loud enough for all present to hear, "Ptolemy, king of Egypt, has sent for my Menander, promising him just about half of his kingdom." And as I spoke, I shook and brandished in my hand the letter with the royal seal. "Do you find any pleasure in being left behind," they said. I had not thought of that, Menander. I couldn't believe, — no, by no manner of means could I believe that Menander would or could ever leave his Glycera behind in

Athens, and enjoy alone in Egypt regal honors and all the treasures of the earth.

The trust that she reposes in Menander forbids her to dream of the possibility that he could ever do without her. If the Egyptians wish to behold Menander, they must come to Athens to Glycera's.

For what is Menander without Glycera, who arranges the masks for him, puts on the robes, stands in the wings squeezing her fingers and all a-tremble until the theatre bursts out into applause. That is the moment when I recover myself and embrace you and hold that sacred head within my arms. The reason, Menander, that I told my friends of my joy at that time was this — not Glycera alone but even kings across the sea are in love with you, and fame has spread your virtues abroad in foreign lands.

Then there rises immediately within her the thought that her own selfishness may deter the object of her love from his own enjoyment. She determines then to efface herself and bid him god-speed. But she cannot let him go.

I will not leave you. Don't think that I merely say this. I could not leave you if I would. No. I will leave my mother and my sisters, and will sail with you. I am a good sailor, I know, and if you become sick when the oars break, and the waves run high, I will comfort you. Like an Ariadne, though without a thread, I will guide you, not Dionysus but the servant and prophet of Dionysus.

In the next moment, however, a mood of uncertainty settles upon her. Menander's happiness, she believes, is staked on her and on his plays, and is not conditioned by abundance of treasures or riches. She fluctuates between urging him to go and begging him to remain. Their happiness is more secure in Athens. Yet the thought of the hatred with which she would be visited by his relatives and fellow-citizens for her undue influence in retaining him in Athens, prompts her to leave the question to arbitration. She first proposes leaving the matter to friends to decide. Then distrusting human counsel, she suggests sending to the oracle at Delphi to learn whether it is wiser for them both to go or to stay. Finally her superstition gets the better of her and she proposes recourse to witchcraft. Meanwhile her moods follow one another with great rapidity. At one moment she writes:

If you are earnestly trying to banish from your thoughts me and the Piraeus, your country seat, Munychia, and everything else, little by little, — no, I cannot do it, nor can you who are so closely joined to me, —

And the next moment with rapid alternation of feeling she adds:

So then, my love, try to come with all speed to the city, so that if you should change your mind about your visit to the king, you may get ready the comedies which will most please Ptolemy. . . . I do beg you, Menander, by all means to prepare that play in which you have portrayed me, so that even if I am not present there with you, I may through you complete the voyage to Ptolemy.

But this intention not to accompany Menander is

merely a passing fancy. She cannot stifle her love for him, and she closes her letter by saying:

You shall not leave your true love behind. Until you come to me from the Piraeus, I shall be learning how to steer a boat and keep the watch, that with my own hands I may guide you across quiet seas, if you think it wise to go. May Heaven grant that what we do be for the best.

The letter shows a careful and delicate portrayal of a character dramatically conceived and well sustained throughout. It affords such a genuine insight into the intricacies, the faint alarms, and the fluctuations of a woman's emotions as to indicate that Alciphron could break loose at times from the trammels that rhetoric imposed, and envisage his characters. Had he thrown such a spirit and manner into the rest of his work, he would occupy a much higher position in literature.

IV

GREEK AND ROMAN ASCETIC TENDENCIES

By CLIFFORD HERSCHEL MOORE

GREEK AND ROMAN ASCETIC TENDENCIES

I

SELF-DISCIPLINE and self-denial for religious ends are practices which we do not ordinarily associate with the Greeks and Romans. It is indeed true that the Greeks more than most peoples ancient or modern, long found satisfaction in the enjoyment of living, unhampered by severe restrictions; self-restraint they prized chiefly for its practical value; in the teachings of Socrates, temperance, "preëminent of virtues," had an immediate ethical aim. But the later philosophic schools, in which philosophy became more and more the hand-maid of religion, consciously endeavored to uproot the innate passions and affections, that the soul of man might grow unhampered toward the divine. The firmness of character, the even balance (*constantia*), which was one of the chief virtues of the Romans, was due to that people's inborn genius for control and orderly rule, and did not have its origin in any religious impulse. Yet at a comparatively early period the Greeks became familiar with certain ascetic practices intended to serve religious ends; and if among the earlier Romans asceticism had no place apart from a few prohibitions of a primitive sort, none the less the western part of the Roman world was destined in due season to prove itself a ready pupil of Greece and the nearer East. It is my purpose in the present paper to sketch the chief lines of the development of ascetic tendencies among the Greeks and Romans from the time when these tendencies first appeared down to the period when an extreme asceticism manifested itself in the Christian church. In this study no sharp distinction will be made between philosophic and religious thought, for apart from the truism that philosophy and religion can never long be separated, it is a fact that classical antiquity made no serious attempt to divorce them.

It is important at the outset to have clearly before our minds what we mean by asceticism and ascetic practices. To-day these expressions always have primarily a negative signification: an ascetic is one who practises unusual or excessive abstinence, self-denial, or self-mortification. But although it is true that in every form of religious asceticism the negative or prohibitive elements have always had a considerable place, we must still remember that the Greek word *ascesis* ($\overset{\text{'}}{\alpha}\sigma\kappa\eta\sigma\iota\varsigma$) for many centuries had a positive rather than a negative connotation, meaning as it does nothing but "practice," "training," "exercise." It was applied especially to the training of the athlete, but was naturally transferred in course of time from the training of the body to the training of the soul, so that the Greeks spoke of a spiritual as well as a physical *ascesis*. Yet since the athlete to develope his body must not only practise certain exercises but also refrain from whatever may hinder his physical development, the word came to carry with it those negative ideas which are most prominent to our modern minds. It must be repeated, however, that to the Greeks the word *ascesis* signified a positive fully as much as a negative exercise, at least until the latest period; and this must here be emphasized since we shall be obliged in the course of our discussion to say much of the prohibitions and abstentions which were taught and practised, because these are the manifestations of asceticism which are most easily apprehended.

Among the Greeks and Romans, as among other peoples, prohibitions are of two classes, which however cannot always be clearly distinguished. The first includes all those prohibitions against specific persons, things, or acts, the origin of which is often lost in antiquity. Later times frequently attributed these taboos, as we now usually denominate them, to some experience real or imagined, or sought to explain them by myth or by rationalization. The second class of prohibitions comprises those which are due to reflection of a higher order, to a consideration of the nature of man, of his relation to divinity, and frequently of a future life. Many of the restrictions which belong to this second class are nothing but primitive taboos, employed with a conscious religious purpose. The significant fact is that they belong to a rule of conduct, being operative over a considerable period or throughout life, and that they are believed to promote the spiritual life of the individual, rather than simply to secure him from injury at the hands of some baneful or angry divinity. This second class of prohibitions will occupy most of our attention, but both Greece and Rome show many restrictions of a primitive sort. These are generally common taboos, like those associated with birth and death. The priests naturally were most subject to restrictions; our oldest example is furnished by the ancient interpreters of the oracle at Dodona, the Selloi, who were apparently forbidden to sleep in beds or to wash their feet. But the specific taboos in Greece vary so much from place to place that it is impossible to give any general account of them. Among the Romans, the Fetials were forbidden to kill their victim with a metal knife, but must use the flint of the stone age; often vessels made on the potter's wheel were taboo in ritual, as were mills in the Vestal's preparation of the flour for their sacred cakes. The fire of Vesta could be renewed only by the primitive method of rubbing two pieces of wood together. Of all the Roman sacred officials the priest of Jupiter was most subject to restrictions; with his wife he was bound by a complex of taboos too large to be enumerated here. Taboos against foods also existed in many places in Greece, but fasting was by no means common. Yet it was required

in the worship of Demeter at the Thesmophoria and in
the mysteries. It was wholly absent from the older Roman ritual, but was introduced in the worship of the
Greek Ceres, and was required by many Oriental 'cults.
Chastity was occasionally imposed: among the Greeks
for instance on the matrons at the Thesmophoria; the
most notable Roman example is the familiar case of the
Vestals, who were bound by their vows for thirty years.
Yet in spite of the fact that all these cases are concerned
with religion, none of the taboos mentioned were imposed with the intent to secure thereby spiritual edification. We must turn therefore to that other class of prohibitions which had such aims.

The earliest ascetic practices properly so called which
we shall consider were those connected with a great
religious and an important philosophic development —
I mean the rise of the Orphic Sect and of Pythagoreanism.
Both belong to the sixth century B.C.; both were inseparably connected with that growth of reflective thought
which was the most striking and fruitful development
of the seventh and sixth centuries before our era. Reflective thought first shows itself clearly in the poems
of Hesiod; it gave rise to elegiac poetry, whose distich
was in its very essence the sententious record of reflection, and to those forms of lyric poetry which expressed
the personal sentiments of the individual; it produced
philosophy, man's attempt to solve the universe; and
finally it stimulated a new religious movement. By the

seventh century B.C. men had come to believe in a system
of divine punishments and rewards, and to conceive of
right and wrong in a way unknown to the Homeric
poems. A new stress was laid on ceremonial purity;
a longing for future happiness had come to the surface
of Greek thought and with it a belief that such immortality was attainable. The outlet for this religious longing was found in the religion of Dionysus as incorporated
in the tenets of the Orphic Sect.

Dionysus came comparatively late into Greek religion. In the Homeric epics he is not a member of the
Olympic circle. Tradition has preserved many stories
which bear witness to the opposition which his rites en-
countered, the most notable of which are those of the
Thracian king Lycurgus, of the daughters of Minyas at
Orchomenus, of Pentheus at Thebes, and of the Proe-
tides at Tiryns. The newcomer, like Ares and the Muses,
was a Thracian; his cult spread slowly to the south in
the period following that represented in the Homeric
poems. Now we learn from competent testimony that
certain Thracian peoples not only held to a kind of mo-
notheism, but also believed that at death men went to
live with their god, not in a shadowy and cheerless existence as in Homeric thought, but in a conscious and a
happier life than they had known in the flesh; furthermore a foretaste of that immortality could be obtained
in this life when the individual, possessed by a divine
madness, in ecstasy, had freed his soul from the bonds

of the body so that for the time it saw divine visions and gained unity with God, with Dionysus. This divine madness was stimulated by wine, by the mystic dance, and by wild music. We can easily understand the horror with which the Greeks first regarded the extravagances of the Bacchanal rout, which the excited participants pursued all unconscious of time or place, superior to the usual limitations of mortal powers and sensibilities, until at last they sank exhausted to the ground. This and the horrible rending of wild beasts, whose raw flesh was devoured by the devotees, must have shocked the earliest Hellenic spectators. Yet they realized sooner or later that there were noble possibilities in this madness, that the bacchant seemed for the time to gain new and superhuman powers, that the reveller was freed from the complex tangle of daily life and rose to unity with all nature which joined in the worship of its one supreme lord, Dionysus, in union with whom the devotee received a foretaste of immortality. This common worship is described by Euripides in his *Bacchae:*

"There
Through the appointed hour, they made their prayer
And worship of the Wand, with one accord
Of heart, and cry 'Iacchos, Bromios, Lord,
God of god born!' And all the mountain felt
And worshipped with them; and the wild things knelt,
And ramped and gloried, and the wilderness
Was filled with moving voices and dim stress." [1]

---

[1] Gilbert Murray's translation.

Intelligible as this joy of release and this delight in kinship with nature are to us to-day, we cannot help feeling that the bacchanal revel is as far as possible removed from anything ascetic. Yet the germ of ascetic practice lay precisely here in the notion of the double ego, soul and body, on which was based the idea that the soul might be temporarily made superior to its home in the flesh. This dualistic conception of man's nature was foreign apparently to early Greek thought, but once implanted in the Greek mind by the religion of Diony-sus, it became a most productive concept; without it ascetic practices could hardly have arisen; and the history of such practices is largely the history of this concept.

It was held that the soul, when exalted by the Bacchic rites, united itself with divinity, became indeed itself a god, so that the orgiastic devotee was given the divine name *Bakchos*. This ecstatic temporary experience showed the path which man must follow to secure immortality, permanent union with God: he must free the divine soul from the body, must purify it, that it might enjoy its natural divine life unhampered by earthly dross. Thus Dionysiac religion brought a new religious inspiration to those who were endeavoring to solve the question of their relation to the divine, and gave them a satisfaction which the older gods could not give.

In the sacred myth Dionysus, to whom Zeus had already given the rule of the world, was tricked and attacked by the Titans, the powers opposed to Zeus; in his distress the god changed himself into various forms, finally assuming that of a bull, in which guise he was torn to pieces and devoured by his pursuers; Athena, however, saved his heart and gave it to Zeus, who swallowed it; hence sprang the new Dionysus. The Titans were ultimately destroyed by Zeus. It will be seen at once that this crude myth, like those of Attis, Osiris, and Adonis, was capable of a spiritual interpretation. And such it received: the reborn Dionysus became the god of resurrection and immortality. Thus interpreted the myth was made the basis of belief and of mystic ceremonial; it became the centre of Orphism. Who Orpheus was we cannot say; the ancients called him a Thracian, a magical musician, a priest of Bacchus and founder of the Bacchic rites. Whether he ever actually existed, as has been lately urged, we may well doubt; but we cannot doubt that during the sixth century B.C., there was developed a considerable movement which spiritualized and ennobled the Dionysiac religion, a movement which aimed to secure a purity in this life, from which immortality would follow.

The religion of the Orphics was distinguished from the popular forms of religion in two points: it had a set body of belief — modified unquestionably by time and place — and it also prescribed a method of life, an *ascesis*. To explain the origin of evil and of multiplicity in the world the sect employed the myth which I have given above. According to their doctrine the Titans are the original powers of evil who by tearing in pieces the divine One produce a multiple world; the rebirth of Dionysus is reunion into unity. Man sprang from the ashes of the Titans who had devoured Dionysus, hence he is evil from his birth, his body representing the Titanic elements of his being; his soul however is divine, being of Dionysiac origin, in fact the image of the god (ὁ ἐν ἡμῖν νοῦς Διονυσιακός ἐστι καὶ ἄγαλμα ὄντως τοῦ Διονύσου). In this concept of body and soul as the dual ego, each opposed to the other, the Orphics found naturally the source of man's moral obligation: he must free himself from the evil Titanic element that the Dionysiac part, the soul, may be untrammelled. The body (σῶμα) was thought of as the grave (σῆμα) of the spirit, which there imprisoned suffers until the penalty of sin be paid — an idea which was taken up by Plato and used by the later religious philosophies. Yet the Orphic might not of his own act cast off his body, for a round was prescribed by necessity, through which the soul must pass by successive rebirths, either into other human bodies or into the forms of lower creatures, as a fragment preserved by Proclus says: "Therefore the soul of man changing in the cycles of time enters into various creatures; now it enters a horse, again it becomes a sheep, or a bird dread to see, or again the form of a dog with heavy voice, or as one of the tribe of chill serpents creeps on the sacred ground."

The whole purpose of the Orphic teaching and mysteries was to enable the devotee to hasten the completion of the prescribed cycle and to obtain respite from evil (κύκλου τε λῆξαι καὶ ἀναπνεῦσαι κακότητος); to this end was imposed a course of life, the requirements of which seem trivial to us, for they consisted not in the practice of public or private morality as we understand it, but in the avoidance so far as possible of all that was mortal. The proscriptions were simple. Abstinence from flesh was the severest. Eggs also and beans were forbidden, since they were used in the ritual of the dead; nor might a woollen garment be used to wrap a corpse, for even in the grave man must be free from mortal contagion. Birth and death alike were thought to bring pollution. The words of Euripides' chorus in his *Cretans* might have been sung by the Orphic:

> "Robed in pure white I have borne me clean
> From man's vile birth and coffined clay,
> And exiled from my lips alway
> Touch of all meat where life hath been." [1]

It will be observed that here, as we shall see presently in Pythagoreanism, taboos of a primitive sort were given by symbolism a spiritual value. To the uninitiate they would seem of little worth, but to the devotee their observance meant the ultimate purification and release of his soul from the prison of the body.

[1] This translation is taken from Miss Harrison, *Prolegomena to Greek Religion*, p. 508.

Pythagoreanism was almost contemporaneous with Orphism, and their tenets at many points cannot be distinguished; their most notable agreement is in the doctrine of metempsychosis. The sect which Pythagoras founded at Croton in southern Italy soon after 529 B.C. was like the Orphics a close body to which the applicant was admitted only after his worth had been tested. But the two bodies also differed fundamentally: the Orphics were primarily a religious company of mystics, conscious of the need of spiritual aid, doing penance to purge away their sinful nature, and thus to secure spiritual happiness; the Pythagoreans on the other hand constituted a semi-political order, planned to meet the requirements of organized society, confident of the value of ethical discipline, and devoted to scientific and rationalistic pursuits. Yet no less than the Orphics the Pythagoreans followed an ascetic course. They regarded life as the path of the soul's purification, so that man must strive unceasingly to purify and perfect himself; to "follow God," to become like God, was their first precept. To this end all the discipline of the sect was directed. When an applicant had been adjudged worthy and been admitted to the brotherhood, he was bound to silent obedience, became wholly subject to the established authority. "The master said it" was to be alike his answer and his assurance. The care of the soul was especially enjoined by the founder, who was himself accustomed to sing at dawn, to the accompaniment of the lyre, ancient paeans and such parts of Homer and Hesiod as he judged suited to attune his spirit to the day's task. Reflection and self-examination were required twice daily: on waking the disciple was to ponder on all that the day might bring forth; before sleeping he was to review with care all that he had said and done, testing with himself each word and act. Pythagoras inculcated especially the habit of truth, "for this alone could make men like to God." This regimen of the soul was aided and supplemented by that of the body. Temperance in food and simplicity in dress were required of all; the use of meat was allowed only under fixed conditions, and many seem to have refrained from it entirely. Certain other foods were tabooed, especially beans; and burial in woollen garments was forbidden for the same reason as among the Orphics. How much Pythagoreanism derived from Orphism, how much either or both owed to the East, are questions which cannot be answered to-day. But it is striking that in the sixth century B.C. there arose two sects, one primarily religious, the other of a politico-religious character, both of which employed ascetic practices to train and purify the soul. So far as our knowledge goes, they introduced asceticism to the European world.

Neither Orphics nor Pythagoreans doubted the efficacy of their holy life. Inscribed tablets found in graves of Italy and Crete bear witness to the confidence of the former. "I am a child of Earth and of Starry

Heaven, but my race is of Heaven alone," is a common expression found on them; in one the soul is assured: "Thou art become God from Man"; and in others the soul confidently declares: "I avow that I am of your blessed race. I have paid the penalty for deeds unrighteous . . . I have escaped from the sorrowful weary wheel." A fragment of an Orphic "Descent to Hades" says: "They who are holy in their life beneath the rays of the sun, in death have a gentler lot in the fair meadow by deep-flowing Acheron; but those who have worked evil in insolent pride on earth, are led down under the plain of Cocytus into chill Tartarus." It was only by successive sojourns in Hades, where the soul was purified, and by many lives on earth that the striving spirit attained at last to purity and happiness. The belief of the Pythagoreans is shown by fragments of the Sicilian poet Epicharmus:

> "If thou hast been pious in thy soul,
> No harm at death can befall thee;
> Above in the heavens thy spirit abides."

Again:

> "Holy living is mortal's chief aid on his course."

Many verses from Empedocles also might be quoted in illustration of the Pythagorean and Orphic doctrines of sin and purification.

If we cannot trace the history of Orphism and Pythagoreanism as things apart from the general course of Greek thought, our inability is somewhat due we may be sure to the fact that their fundamental ideas were absorbed and became familiar to the Hellenic world. Probably their communities continued, especially in southern Italy where their existence down to a late period is attested by the tablets from which I have quoted. Under the Roman Empire Pythagoreanism enjoyed a revival, while Orphism was recalled and played an important part in Neoplatonism.

It is not surprising that in the period following directly on the Persian Wars we hear practically nothing of ascetic doctrine or practice at Athens. The enormous stimulus to national pride given by the victory over the Persians, the high confidence in their own powers roused by their growing empire, and the satisfaction with life provided by their increasing wealth, left no class of Athenians in the middle of the fifth century desire or occasion to resort to asceticism; and besides the Eleusinian overshadowed all other mysteries. But when their wealth and empire had wasted away in the disasters of the Peloponnesian War, the rising philosophic movement at Athens gained a new significance. Possibly also the failure of the Orphics to secure a high position among the Athenians was in part due to quackery and superstition, which brought the whole movement into disrepute.

Whatever extravagances Orphism fell to, it must be kept in mind that it had introduced into the European world certain doctrines pregnant with spiritual fruit.

The dualism of sinful body and divine soul, with the consequent obligation on the individual to strive by a holy mode of life, an *ascesis*, to realize his divinity; and the moral use made of belief in the immortality of the soul, spurring man to cleanse his soul, "to fast from sin" (νηστεῦσαι κακότητος) — these doctrines, entangled though they were in myth and ritual, were of great service to the world. It remained for Plato to bring the Orphic seed to fruit by giving an intellectual basis to the doctrine of the divine nature of the soul, which he thus raised out of the plane of mere emotional belief.

II

In the many-sided Plato there is a strong separatist strain. Although he rejected the external and symbolical purifications of the Orphics, he held a doctrine of *ascesis* for spiritual ends which is not without kinship with theirs. This is set forth most clearly in the *Phaedo*, with which parts of the *Republic* and of other dialogues must be read. Like the Orphics Plato attributes evil to the prison-house of the soul, the body — sometimes to the body and the lower part of man's spirit. The soul's rational element, which he calls now "the sovereign part of the soul" or again "the eye of the soul," is for him divine, and it is exactly the possession of this divine element which makes man most human; therefore, he urges, if we yield to ambition and passion, we shall bind fast the chains which hold the soul in ward; if we cherish our mortal nature, we shall destroy our divine, immortal element, which to live must by force of reason move upward and escape from its dungeon. Furthermore, since our very humanity consists in the possession of the divine element in our souls, if we give way to the senses and passions, we shall be false to our true selves. We must rather be true, and by following the life of reason begin an immortality now, so far as we may (ἐφ᾽ ὅσον ἐνδέχεται, ἀθανατίζειν). Here we have a nobler *ascesis* than any proscription of food and dress; but none the less an *ascesis* cogent and necessary. For, as Socrates says in the *Phaedo*, "the soul of the true philosopher thinks that she ought not to resist this deliverance (by philosophy from the passions), and therefore abstains from pleasures and desires and pains and fears so far as she is able; . . . each pleasure and pain is a sort of nail which nails and rivets the soul to the body, until she becomes the body; . . . and from agreeing with the body and having the same delights she is obliged to have the same habits and haunts, and is not likely ever to be pure at her departure."[1] The body therefore is to be mortified for the sake of the soul; all life is to be a "practice of death" (μελέτη θανάτου). This last, however, is no negative doctrine, for if the body be the prison in which the enfettered soul is in danger of death, then what we call death is only the release of the soul into life; the practice of death is actually the practice of life. Plato, no

[1] Jowett's translation.

less than St. Paul, would have men seek to deliver themselves from the body of death by mortifying their earthly members and the deeds of the body that the soul may live. Man's chief good lies in escape from this world into similarity with God; as Socrates in the *Theaetetus* replies to Theodorus: "Since evils have no place among the gods of heaven, they are forced to hover around the earthly nature and this mortal sphere. Therefore we should try to escape with all speed from this world; but escape is likeness to God so far as possible, and likeness to God consists in becoming just and holy under the guidance of reason" (πειρᾶσθαι χρὴ ἐνθένδε ἐκεῖσε φεύγειν ὅτι τάχιστα, φυγὴ δὲ ὁμοίωσις θεῷ κατὰ τὸ δυνατόν ὁμοίωσις δὲ δίκαιον καὶ ὅσιον μετὰ φρονήσεως γενέσθαι.)

If the founder of the Academy thus gave to Greek ethics an ascetic impulse, the same cannot be said of the great teacher in the Lyceum. Aristotle's doctrine of the mean as the path of virtue and piety, the place given in his system to passion and desire, excluded all strenuous *ascesis*: the passions were not to be crushed out, but curbed and brought into subjection to the reasoning will. Of the later philosophic schools none requires long consideration here save that of the Stoics; for in spite of Epicurus' contention that happiness was inseparably linked with reason, so that man might endure bodily torture and yet be happy, his doctrine of hedonism, like that of his predecessor the Cyrenaic Aristippus, was incapable of becoming a practical teacher of severe self-

restraint; and among the Sceptics and those attached
to the Later Academy common sense following the
course of probability and experience led to no extremes
of doctrine or of practice.

But at the same time that Plato was establishing the
Academy, another pupil of Socrates, a certain Antis-
thenes, brought into life a sect which was destined to
have much influence on later practical morals. Antis-
thenes and his followers in the Cynic School, especially
Diogenes, by laying excessive emphasis on the virtue of
the individual soul to the neglect of all external obligations and conventions, led the way logically to separa-
tism; in practice their sectaries often displayed that
absurd ostentation in neglect of person and disregard of
all obligations toward the world which drew on itself the
merited scorn of the satirists, but which nevertheless
fitted the pessimism of the period of decay. But since
their doctrine of virtue as the chief good did not include
the life-giving principle of moral activity, it came to
nought within the sect. Stoicism, however, adopted the
doctrine, gave it vigor by insisting on the exercise of
the will in the practice of virtue, and thereby contributed to the spiritual life of fully five centuries.

The Stoic system made large demand for the subjugation to reason of the individual's will and desire: by
conceiving man's highest duty and chief good to be the
adaptation of his life to the rational order of nature, by
calling on man to live in accordance with nature, i.e. in

agreement with the rational cosmos of which man himself is a rational part, the disciples of Zeno opened the way for a rigorous self-discipline, and tended to force men to resist their natural affections and passions. It is also true that Stoicism was always a practical philosophy which intentionally squared itself with society and everyday life; yet its large resistant and disciplinary elements constantly reasserted themselves so that in the first two centuries of the Roman Empire they had become its dominant features. In the developed system virtue was held to consist in absolute mastery over pain, passion, and desire, and in the complete independence of the philosopher (*sapiens*), who possessing true knowledge of the relations of things and complete moral perception, is thereby himself endowed with perfection. It is this perfection which secures him from want, fear, passion, or weakness; it assures him alone possession of all goods and freedom. The extreme doctrinaire character of this teaching led to many absurdities, at which the common-sense onlookers like Horace had many a gibe. Nevertheless, Stoicism's insistence on moral integrity as the one qualification for useful action and for happiness, logically bound its sectaries to a self-discipline which was rigorous in proportion to their fidelity to the ideal.

Now of all the philosophies which Hellenism passed on to Rome, that of the Porch was most akin to the Roman genius and attracted the largest number of followers. As has just been said, under the Empire, when men, especially the members of the intellectual class, were turned in on themselves by the loss of political freedom, and during no small part of the first century lived in terror of the imperial power, the resistant elements of Stoicism were cherished and developed until the system ended as a moral philosophy. In practice it was by no means extreme; it rather aimed at a practical process of moral edification; it became a religion. When Seneca's detractors charged that his life did not correspond with his teachings, he made the sensible and noble reply: "This is enough for me, to take away each day something from my faults, to rebuke my errors. I have not attained complete moral health, nor shall I ever attain it." The endurance, the self-repression which the later teachers, Seneca, Musonius, Epictetus, and Marcus Aurelius inculcate, does not concern itself so much with particular prohibitions as with abstention in general from entanglement with whatever is external to the real man, with the avoidance of everything which may hamper the freedom of the soul. Seneca, it is true, in his youth was led by his teacher, the Pythagorean Sotion, to refrain from meat for an entire year, until his father's arguments in favor of his health and safety induced him to return to a more normal diet; years later he wrote that at the time he had thought that the vegetarian diet made his mind the quicker, and even then he was not ready to deny that this was so. From another master, Attalus, Seneca

learned to accustom himself to a hard mattress, which
he continued to use in old age. The same teacher taught
him to scorn riches, all pleasures of the senses, in fact
everything that was not useful to the philosopher. If the
pupil when old was obliged to confess that he had not
observed all these prohibitions, he still could claim that
he had practised certain abstentions: he had always refrained from luxuries of the table, such as oysters and
mushrooms, from wine, hot baths, and unguents—
trifling and insignificant matters to our minds perhaps,
but not insignificant when we remember the character
of Seneca and his high position in a dissolute and luxurious court. That his daily fare was frugal was proved
by his own body, which, according to Tacitus, was found
at his death to be wasted by the meagre sustenance he
had given it. These particular abstentions were, however, only by-products, so to speak, of the Stoic doctrine
which is repeated again and again by the great representatives whom I have named above. "Endure and ab-
stain" (ἀνέχου καὶ ἀπέχου), thus Epictetus gives the key-
note of later Stoicism. In the exercise of endurance
and abstention lay the whole art of living; spiritual exercise, *ascesis*, is to be the constant occupation of the
individual. Epictetus has indeed a special chapter
entitled "On Exercise," in which he declares that we
must limit our exercise to those things which fall within
the power of our will, since on these alone can we practise desire and aversion, and thus train ourselves to live

free from all restraint. Now freedom, which is itself
happiness and peace, is the whole object of man's self-
exercise; and freedom consists solely in the knowledge
how to live and in the exercise of that knowledge. Man
therefore must not desire or exercise himself in the pursuit of health, honor, riches, or anything which may
depend on the will of another; he must feel an aversion
for, and exercise himself against, all passions, sense of
wrong, fear of men or gods, and the dread of death. Only
thus may one attain to freedom and live in the liberty of
the will. In this sense man must attach himself to God,
and being of the same mind with God, accept the divine
will with tranquillity and joy.

In this practical and noble doctrine of edification, of
which I have given only an imperfect sketch, we see a
positive and a negative side: man must train his soul in
the exercise of virtue within the sphere which lies under
the control of his will; he must cut himself off from all
that lies outside such control. Yet ostentation was to be
avoided; one was not to exhibit his proficiency. An interesting glimpse of the practice of the great is given us by
Seneca who reminds Lucilius that many have in their
palaces cells to which they secretly retire, and on a diet
of coarse bread, dressed in a poor garment, and sleeping
on a humble cot, train themselves to meet misfortune
bravely, even as a soldier trains himself to meet the
foe. The teacher urges his friend to train himself by
similar means that he may learn to be satisfied with little

and to know that happiness does not depend on great estate.

It was inevitable that with this emphasis on the opposition of the spirit and the flesh which lies behind the Stoic doctrine, there should arise a scorn of the body which finds its strongest expression in Marcus Aurelius. "What am I?" the Emperor asks himself, and answers with a quotation from Epictetus: "A poor soul, burdened with a corpse"; again, "I am of body and soul. To the body all things are indifferent; it has no power to differentiate. To the intellect all things are indifferent, save its own activities; and its own activities are all within its own control"; and again the Emperor exhorts himself: "Flesh, Breath, and the Inner Self — that is all. Good-bye, my books! strain after them no more; they are not your portion. As in the near presence of death, despise poor flesh — this refuse of blood and bones, this web and tissue of nerves and veins and arteries. Breath too! What is it? A puff of wind never the same, but every moment exhaling and again inhaled. Last comes the Inner Self — on that stake all." [1]

Although Stoicism was the most important of the religious philosophies in the western half of the Empire at this period, it was not alone in asserting that edification of the soul was the aim of all philosophy, nor was it alone in coming through the ancient opposition of flesh and spirit to despise the body. The extraordinary relig-

[1] Rendall's translation.

ious movement which had been growing during the last
two centuries before the beginning of the Christian era
— a movement filled with eager longing for the assurance
of spiritual salvation — had revived the mystic tendency
which was always strong among the Greeks, and had
communicated it to the Romans. The result in popular
religion we shall consider later; in philosophy it called
men away from the resort to reason or to the senses
which had distinguished the schools immediately after
Aristotle. In the case of Stoicism it led to a practical
morality; at Alexandria, the meeting place of Oriental
and Western thought, it led to new philosophic movements which combined religion and mysticism in a way
unknown before. One of the sects, the Neopythagoreans,
returning to the mystic symbolism of the earlier school,
endeavored to unite this with the teachings of Plato into
a scientific system. Judeo-Alexandrian philosophy, of
which Philo is the chief representative, tried to combine
the religious doctrines of Judaism with Platonism. Both
schools adopted in different degrees the Platonic doctrine of a transcendental god; both emphasized the
opposition of flesh and spirit, the spirit by nature pure
and divine, the flesh base and defiling. For both also the
aim of philosophy was to attain to association with God;
but to draw near to God in his remote transcendence,
every means was to be taken to free the spirit from the
hampering body in which it dwells.

The Neopythagoreans observed the prohibitions imposed by the earlier school: much stress was laid on purificatory baths, baptisms, and white garments; all contact with the dead or with an impure person was to be avoided; and certain foods were forbidden. Celibacy was approved, although not imposed. Fidelity to the marriage bond was required, and sexual indulgence within this bond allowed only for the begetting of children. Of more importance, however, than these prescriptions and prohibitions was the emphasis laid on sanctity. The saint became the ideal. To this position Pythagoras had naturally been raised in the course of centuries; the model in later time was furnished by Apollonius of Tyana, who lived in the first century of our era and may have come under the influence of Eastern asceticism. The historical Apollonius is lost to us in the cloud of marvellous legend with which he was invested in the century following his death; yet our loss is more than recompensed by the knowledge we gain of the ideal of later Pythagoreanism. Apollonius was regarded as one filled with divine inspiration, who by virtue of the revelation given to him stood far above ordinary mortals, a worker of miracles. His life was most simple: his food was bread, fruits, and ordinary herbs; water was his only drink; he practised silence, and neglected his person. His mission, according to his biographer, was to free men through true philosophy from the prison of the body; he demanded a righteousness far above the ordinary morality of correct actions; he apparently taught that purity of life and true wisdom, in which lay the proper worship of the divine, could raise man to supernatural power and sanctity. Thus Neopythagoreanism not only gave an added emphasis to asceticism but also fixed in the religious life a new ideal, that of the saint who receives direct revelation from God.

Judeo-Alexandrian philosophy went even farther than Neopythagoreanism. According to Philo, its chief exponent, man is wholly sunk in sin from which his unaided efforts can never free him. This sinful condition is due to the voluntary descent of the soul from the super-sensuous sphere to this world of the senses where it has entered into union with the body, its horrible prison, which it is doomed to drag with it on earth. Unreasoning passion and lust belong to the body, but divinity to the reasoning soul. As a practical guide the ethical teachings of the Stoics were adopted, at least externally. But Philo would go further than the Stoics. Virtue for him as for them consists in pure morality: all passions and desires are to be crushed out that man may attain to complete dispassionateness ($\dot{a}\pi\dot{a}\theta\epsilon\iota a$), not to that middle state of moderate freedom from the passions which was the balance struck by the Stoic between his ideal and the practice of the ignorant. It is true that Philo also made concessions to the actual world. He seems to have recognized that political life was a necessity, in which however the wise man would not lose himself; rather he should wash away the defilements of the soul and prove his virtue in affairs before he could pass on to the contemplative life, which is the highest activity. Yet Philo would not have wholly rejected the description of the lovers of virtue, i.e. the true philosophers, which he puts into the mouths of those who defend the care of the person and worldly ambition: "Those who are called lovers of virtue are usually without reputation, despised of men, humble, needy, more dishonored than slaves, dirty, pale and emaciated, always facing hunger, sick, practitioners of death (μελετῶντες ἀποθνῄσκειν)." The irony of this description is shown by the last phrase which he borrows from Plato, and which we have discussed above. Such poor creatures philosophers may seem, Philo would answer, but in reality, in their pursuit of a noble ideal, they know that joy which every wise man feels, "for he rejoices in himself, not in his surroundings." Logically Philo should have favored a withdrawal from the world into separatist communities, such as the Essenes had already established, but like the Neopythagoreans and Stoics, he was held back by the inherited bonds of society from taking that step.

It will be felt that between Philo's doctrine of man's helplessness in sin and the Stoic doctrine of obligation to free the soul by subduing the sinful body, there is a serious gap. Man, because he is sinner, cannot fulfil his obligation to free himself from sin. The only possible bridge across the gap was found in the activity of a higher power which may lend man the strength to free himself.

Salvation then is an act of grace, a revelation from God.

So Neopythagoreanism, Judeo-Alexandrian philosophy, and we may add Platonism in the first two centuries of our era, all had a strong mystical character. In every school the older belief in the self-sufficiency of man in his warfare against the passions had been replaced by faith in divine revelation as a means of salvation. Even the Stoic had come to look for external aid. All systems inculcated scorn of the flesh, despite of the world with its vanities and temptations; all insisted on a constant exercise in crushing out the passions and thus freeing the soul. In short the dominant philosophies of this period gave a new emphasis to asceticism.

III

But at this point the question may reasonably be asked how far this scorn and mortification of the flesh, these rigorous exercises of the soul were confined to a select few whose noble aspirations lifted them above the mass. It must be granted that the ideal and the practice of the devout philosopher may well seem to be poor evidence of the sentiments of the common people. But, on the other hand, we must remember that before the second century of our era philosophy had ceased to be primarily speculative, had become indeed the art of life, so that it might be embraced even by the unlettered. Epictetus in fact warns against the study of written precepts, and

Marcus Aurelius, in a passage quoted above, exhorts his soul to bid farewell to books. We have direct evidence, however, in the popular religions of the period, and to these we must now turn.

Her geographical situation and commercial relations exposed Greece to the religious influences of Asia Minor and of Egypt. In the earlier period she was able to absorb and hellenize all cults from abroad, but by the fourth century B.C. her vitality was weakening and the gods of the Orient and Egypt came in too great numbers to be nationalized. Before 333-32 B.C. a shrine of Isis had been established in Attica by state permission; after the conquests of Alexander a crowd of foreign divinities poured into Greek lands. The island of Delos, owing to its commercial position, became a great centre for these cults and played an important part in transmitting them to the West. As early as the second century B.C. Isis and her attendant divinities were worshipped in southern Italy; in Cicero's day she was established on the very Capitol, from which no official efforts could permanently dislodge her. Already in 204 B.C. the Great Mother of the Gods had been brought from Asia Minor by the state's official action. In fact by the close of the first century of the Empire a large number of Oriental and Egyptian gods were domiciled in Italy, where they claimed a multitude of devotees among the Italian, as well as foreign, population. Most of these cults had certain common characteristics which marked them

off from the official religion of the state: they were cosmopolitan, open to all; each had its priests, eager propa-
gandists devoted to the divine service; the followers of
each formed a body which had been set apart from the
rest of the world, consecrated by a mystic initiation to
which they had been admitted only after they had observed for a fixed period certain prohibitions.

Through the fortunate circumstance that Apuleius of
Madaura has left us an account of his initiation into the
rites of Isis we know these in considerable detail. The
prospective initiate was obliged to wait until the goddess
through her priest had made known her willingness to
receive him. When the divine consent had been granted,
the novice was given a purificatory bath, which was followed by prayer and baptism; he was then brought to the
temple where, before the image of the goddess, he was
charged to refrain from wine, meat, and all luxuries of
the table for ten days. When these prohibitions had been
faithfully observed, the initiation proper began. The
same requirements were made at each of the two succeeding degrees. The shaven head, the mark branded
on the forehead of the priests at least, the linen dress,
participation in daily matins and vespers at the shrines
of the goddess, all marked the initiates as a separate
body apart; the devotees had indeed entered on the
Isiac life which gave them happiness here and assurance
of salvation hereafter. The purpose of the bath, baptism, and fasting before initiation, as of the sexual con-

tinence imposed on women during the annual festival of the goddess, was to purify the body that the soul might be free to receive the divine influence. There is operative here then that same dualism of flesh and spirit which we have found in all our previous considerations.

Nowhere does this dualism appear more clearly than in the religion of Mithras, which adds to it as an effective element the doctrine of the active presence in the world of contending powers of good and evil; the servants of Ahriman, defeated by Mithras in their original effort to destroy the progenitors of man, continually endeavor to drag mortals down while Mithras helps his faithful followers on to victory. Life in the Mithraic system is a continual struggle against the powers of evil toward the goal of purity that the soul, the divine essence in man, may finally rise to the celestial regions. Mithraism therefore called not for a life of contemplation but for one of constant effort; it was suited to men of action, to a soldiery, and therein lies in part the explanation of its popularity among the armies of the Empire. In the Mithraic community there were no less than seven grades of initiation; in the passage from one degree to another, purificatory baths, prayers, abstinence from certain foods, and continence were required; the courage and endurance of the initiate were also tested; an oath was exacted of him; and there is some reason to believe that on reaching the third grade he was branded on the forehead like the priests of Isis. The beginnings at least of religious communities were made. Tertullian speaks of "continents" and "virgins" among the Mithraists, which may point to an incipient monasticism, such as was found among the priests of Isis and Sarapis. The Mithraic devotee was encouraged in his fidelity, given wisdom and strength for his struggle against the minions of Ahriman by reunions with his fellows in the Mithraic chapel and by a holy communion which with consecrated loaf and cup recalled the banquet instituted by Mithras before his ascension.

We can hardly doubt that similar obligations were laid on the devotees in many, if not most, of the Oriental cults of the Empire. In moral value they varied of course all the way from the extravagances of a debased superstition to the noble practices of an enlightened religion. But self-mutilation and flagellation, as practised in the worship of the Great Mother, of Bellona, and of the Syrian Goddess; baptisms in the blood of the sacred victim; abstinence from proscribed foods, continence, lustral baths, and all the prerequisites of initiation; the avoidance of everything in dress which might defile the wearer; the loftiest exercise of the soul — all aimed at the same end: the subjugation of the sinful body and the freeing of the soul in its effort to attain to an ideal of purity, whatever that ideal might be. The aim of religion had been vastly changed; formerly it had not clearly raised the question of moral worth, but now, recognizing the presence of good and evil in man's

environment as well as in the constitution of man himself, conscious of the endless conflict of the divine against
the powers of darkness, and influenced by the vast
changes which had taken place in the social and political organism, religion had come to set moral worth above
all things. The ideal for man, or for God, was no longer
power or dominion apart from moral excellence, but for
both alike purity and sanctity. It cannot be denied that
childish superstitions and debased practices often existed side by side with the nobler forms of religious
effort and that the ideal of sanctity was by no means
always such as we cherish to-day, but nevertheless it is
true that by the second century of our era we find the
religious devotee and the philosopher at one: both alike
stake all on the Inner Self.

We have now seen that both popular religion and
philosophy had come to depend in no small degree on
asceticism to purify and free the soul; and those schools
which had introduced the belief that divine help was
necessary to assist man in his *ascesis*, diminished no
whit the obligation on the individual to strive unceasingly to overcome the evil within him. We have also
recognized that after Alexander the tendency to require
a severer asceticism had grown until sanctity was the
ideal of the nobler part of paganism. I have spoken of the
canonization of Pythagoras. Plato also was early regarded as more than human by his followers; among the
Neoplatonists his regular epithet was "the divine" — an

epithet more than merely honorific. I have mentioned also Apollonius of Tyana who was made by the Neopythagoreans the incarnation of a religious ideal. The readiness with which men in the second century attributed to individuals a superhuman position and power is also shown by the divine honors paid to Alexander of Abonuteichus, that founder of shrines and oracles. The habit of worshipping the saints in the third century is well illustrated by the much quoted case of the Emperor Alexander Severus, who placed in his private chapel the images of his ancestors, of his better predecessors in the imperial office, and also of "the noblest spirits of the past." Among these were Apollonius, Christ, Abraham, Orpheus, and Alexander the Great. The last had his place neither as the conqueror of the world nor as the founder of a new world-order, but as the powerful sage, the perfect prince, the model of virtue and courage, which myth and legend had made him. Before this strange company of the benefactors of mankind the Emperor in secret found spiritual inspiration. We need not suppose that the veneration of such a fantastic collection of saints was common; but the devotion of the Emperor to this strange company after all does testify to the spirit of his age, which believed that by discipline, self-imposed and divinely aided, man could raise himself into the ranks of the divine.

The last great philosophic system to employ asceticism in the Greco-Roman world was early Neoplaton-

ism. In the teaching of Plotinus, the founder of the
school, it occupied a secondary position. Yet his own
practice shows that the ascetic regimen was the natural
one for the philosopher at this period, for Porphyry tells
us that his master remained unmarried, abstained from
animal food, lived in the simplest way, and so despised
his body that he seemed to be ashamed of its possession.
When one of his disciples, a senator Rogantianus, freed
his slaves, gave away his property, laid down his pretor-
ship, took to a wandering life of fasting and dependence,
and finally reduced himself by his self-imposed priva-
tions to a state of semi-helplessness, Plotinus not only
approved but praised him. If it had not been for the
opposition of the envious, with the help of the Emperor
Gallienus and his consort he would have founded a
Platonopolis in Campania, where with his disciples he
would have formed a separate community, living according to Plato's *Laws* and devoted to the philosophic life.

Porphyry, however, the pupil and successor of Plotinus, emphasized almost exclusively the practical life;
for him man's proper care was anxiety for the safety of
his own soul. He taught that men must regard their
bodies as garments, which not only burden but actually
defile them, and which they like athletes must lay aside
that naked and unclothed they may enter the stadium to
contend in the Olympia of the soul (γυμνοὶ δὲ καὶ ἀχίτωνες
ἐπὶ τὸ στάδιον ἀναβαίνωμεν τὰ τῆς ψυχῆς Ὀλύμπια ἀγωνισόμε-
νοι). He held that man's approach to God is directly

proportioned to the freedom which man obtains from the clogging association with the body. "The more we turn toward that which is mortal," he says, "the more we unfit our minds for the infinite grandeur, and the more we withdraw from attachment to the body, in just that measure we approach the divine." Love of body and love of God cannot exist together according to Porphyry's view, but the former must be eradicated. Like Plato, he aims at the death of all sensuous pleasures or rather at the death of all desire for such pleasures, that by such death the soul may be liberated. Naturally the ascetic means by which Porphyry would secure this liberation are the same that we have constantly met; he differs from his predecessors only in the emphasis which he lays on abstention. Everything was to be avoided which can excite the senses: complete abstention from sexual indulgence was most desirable; horse-races, exhibitions of athletes, and similar shows were to be shunned; and since meat feeds the passions, a vegetarian diet was to be adopted. The fact that the treatise, *On Abstinence from Animal Food*, was addressed as an argument to a brother Firmus who had fallen away from vegetarianism, tends to show that such was the accustomed regimen of the school.

With Porphyry *ascesis* as a moral discipline reaches its height. His successor Iamblichus turned his attention to the development of a theological system for paganism; and the later Neoplatonists spent their efforts in other directions.

IV

We have thus surveyed in outline the growth of ascetic tendencies among the Greeks and Romans for fully nine hundred years. We have seen these begin among Orphics and Pythagoreans, the first sects to grasp the meaning of the dualism of flesh and spirit, gain significance in Plato and the later philosophic schools, until during the last three centuries of the period we have considered, asceticism was the normal regimen for the philosopher of nearly every sect. This development in philosophy was paralleled by the course of popular religion from the time when Oriental cults spread to the West. Although the extremer forms of asceticism were never practised by large numbers in Greco-Roman paganism, nevertheless it has been made evident, I trust, that the practice of subjugating the flesh by the repression of the passions, by fasts, and by varied means of discipline that the soul might be free to live and approach the divine, was widely established by the third century of our era.

But at the same time that the later philosophies were developing and Eastern pagan cults were establishing themselves in the West, Christianity also was spreading throughout the Roman Empire. At first it stood apart from the political and social worlds, or rather maintained a passive attitude toward them; but it was inevitable that as soon as this attitude was abandoned, two opposite tendencies should appear: the one due to an effort to come into relation with pagan society, resulted in the secularization of the church; the other, stimulated by the desire to withdraw from the world, found its expression in Christian asceticism. Now asceticism was on the whole foreign to primitive Christianity as it was to Judaism until after the capture of Jerusalem by Titus. It is true that a Jewish sect, the Essenes, had formed separatist communities as early as the second century B.C., but the Essenes were not strictly speaking a national development so much as the product of Hellenistic influences, especially Orphic and Pythagorean, acting on Jewish stock. The same is apparently true of the Therapeutae, who are described by Philo as following an ascetic life in Egypt. But neither of these sects seems to have influenced Judaism or early Christianity to any great extent. In the teachings of Jesus there is little that points toward asceticism: his command to the rich young man to sell all that he had and give to the poor, his exhortation to his disciples to sell their possessions and give alms, to lay up treasures in heaven, and a single saying in which he seems to regard celibacy as a higher state than marriage, are practically all his recorded teachings which can be interpreted as favoring asceticism. Certain passages in the Pauline epistles contain more pronounced doctrine. In the Epistle to the Romans the sinful body is opposed to the "inward man," the "will," more than once, a doctrine which, as

our previous considerations have shown, was nothing
new to the writer of the epistle or to those to whom it
was addressed. In his letter to the Corinthians Paul
expresses his approval of virginity, yet at the same time
emphatically declares that the marriage state is not sinful; and in the Epistle to Timothy celibacy and vegetarianism are distinctly combatted. In general, therefore, we may maintain that the teaching of primitive
Christianity did not favor asceticism; it rather inculcated purity of life, deeds of kindliness, the unselfish
fulfillment of social duties, and similar virtues, which
are fundamentally at variance with a life isolated from
the active world and given to self-contemplation and to
self-abasement. Yet Christianity could not escape the
environment into which it had come. The individual
Christian felt the same anxiety and distress as the pagan
over economic and social decay, the same alarm over the
pressure of the barbarians on the weakened Roman
Empire; he was liable also to be the victim of persecu-
tion; in joining the Christian community he had not laid
aside the belief that by checking and subduing the passions of the body he could free his soul. Furthermore,
the belief in the speedy return of Christ and the immi-
nent approach of the end of the world soon had a mighty
influence on Christian thought and practice. It is not
surprising then that we find as early as the second century a new value laid by Christians on poverty, fasts,
and chastity. During this century also the custom of

fasting on Wednesday and Friday, the *dies stationum*, was established; many bound themselves to perpetual virginity so that an order was almost formed within the church; and riches were regarded as incompatible with the highest Christian character. Furthermore, certain sects arose which laid extravagant stress on asceticism. Such were the Gnostics, Montanists, and Encratites, who became dangerous to the church before the end of the second century; in the third Manicheism added its threats from the East. Although the church was able formally to free itself from these heresies, it could not escape their influence. And besides, the disasters of the latter half of the third century inevitably stimulated a radical asceticism. Men felt a desire to turn away from the evidences of political and moral decay around them toward self-contemplation, from the cares of the external world to the peace of inward experience. It was in the intellectual centre of the Empire, in Egypt, at once the oldest part of the Empire and the place where the decay of the ancient order was most keenly felt, that extreme asceticism showed itself most strongly. The catechistic schools of Alexandria were filled with those who sought to escape from the world, while at the same time the number of those who endeavored to find peace in solitude rapidly increased. The earliest gathering of Christian ascetics was that which formed about Hieracas at Leontopolis in the Nile delta at the close of the third century. When a considerable number had associated themselves with some eminent anchoret, as many did with St. Antony a generation later, the beginning of monasticism was at hand; this was definitely established when Pachomius brought such a gathering of individuals into a community and gave them rules for admission and for conduct. Within a hundred years monasticism had spread to Western Europe.

The intellectual basis, however, of Christian asceticism had been already given by the great theologians of the Alexandrian schools, Clement and Origen, who established as a Christian ideal that life which, free from earthly passion and desire, withdrawn from the world, finds its rest in God. But it was pagan teaching which had given the theologians this ideal of the ascetic saint. The warrant of Christian asceticism, therefore, came primarily neither from Judaism nor from the teachings of Christ and the apostles, but from Hellenistic philosophy, from the tenets of the later Pythagoreans and Platonists, even as the Christian practice of asceticism had arisen out of the religious practice of Greco-Roman paganism.

V

SOME ASPECTS OF AN ANCIENT ROMAN CITY

By MORRIS HICKY MORGAN

SOME ASPECTS OF AN ANCIENT
ROMAN CITY

IT is related that Sir Walter Scott, during his visit
to Pompei, was frequently heard to exclaim, "The
City of the Dead," with no other remark. So difficult
was it even for his marvellous imagination to conjure
up the activities of living men and all the bustle of a
city in that abandoned spot. Many another traveller
and many professed antiquarians have found themselves unable to escape from the shadow of death which,
in spite of all that the skilful methods of modern ex-
cavation and restoration have accomplished, still hangs
over these desolated walls. Yet if one turns to ancient
sites where human habitation has never been so rudely
interrupted — to Naples, for instance, or to Rome herself — and strives to picture what kind of life was lived
in such places in the ancient times, one's purpose may
be thwarted, perhaps even more completely, by modern changes which have utterly destroyed what existed
in the past or altered it almost beyond recognition. The
fact of course is that the material remains of Roman
antiquity can never by themselves suffice for a reconstruction of the life of the ancient Romans. Fortunately,
however, the Romans have left us a literature as well,
and one who can combine the literary with the material

monuments need not despair of reaching some pretty
definite conclusions regarding many sides of that van-
ished life. Even of the outer aspects of city life, about
which we might not hope for much from a literature
written when guide books were unknown, more than a
little is thus to be learned, so that one may speak with
some confidence about them. What, then, were the aspects of a Roman city during the late Republic and the
early Empire, and how did cities in those days differ
in appearance from the cities of modern times?

When one approaches a modern city, one observes
that the skyline is broken by the spires and domes of
churches, by tall chimneys, and often in recent years
by the tops of those lofty buildings which we term
"sky-scrapers." One sees streamers of black smoke
rising here and there, or a great pall of it overhanging
the whole. Though the ancients sometimes grumbled
about the smoke in their cities, yet they knew nothing
of the real nuisance that has come from soft coal. There
were no spires or tall chimneys in those days. As for
"sky-scrapers," Rome itself had them, but in other
cities the buildings were comparatively low, with flat
or low-peaked roofs. If the practical Vitruvius, the
Augustan architect, congratulated Rome on its ability
to provide for an indefinitely large population by means
of its many floors "high in the air," yet the refined and
luxurious Capuans scoffed at a city, which, unlike
theirs, was "hoisted up and suspended on upper

stories." The skyline of an ancient city was therefore generally unbroken, except that near the centre of the town there would probably be a hill with temples or fortifications on top of it, because the oldest cities were usually founded upon some small hill for purposes of defence.

When one comes near to an American or English city, there is no obstacle to prevent immediate entrance, and even continental cities are sometimes pierced to the very centre by a railway. But in antiquity travellers were stopped at the city wall. This was because the ancient city was twofold, comprising a tract of land which was inhabited and cultivated in times of peace, and a stronghold or walled town into which all the citizens would withdraw for protection in time of war. Exactly the same method of settlement was followed by our ancestors in the different parts of this country, who had their clearings and cultivated fields surrounding the stockade in which they took refuge from the Indians or from each other. The walled town in antiquity was the centre of civic and business life; there the markets were held and public and private business was transacted. Some of the citizens had their houses within, others without, the wall. On approaching an ancient city, therefore, by a well paved Roman road, we should first observe the country houses of the rich and the farmhouses of the lower orders, constituting the suburbs; descending from some hill or crossing a plain there would be one or more aqueducts carrying the water supply from some pure source at a distance from the walls. To-day as we approach Rome by the Appian Way, we see no country houses, for all were destroyed long ago and the Campagna is a great waste; but we do see the ruins of the Claudian aqueduct, one of those enormous stone structures the remains of which are to be seen almost everywhere that Romans built cities, and some of which are still so perfect as to be in use at the present time.

Coming nearer to the city, we should see lines of tombs and family burial lots abutting on each side of the road, as we see them still standing along the road which leads to the Herculaneum gate of Pompei. For the Romans hardly ever allowed burial within the city walls; it took place, whether of bodies, or of ashes after cremation, just outside, and consequently the road for miles from an important city — for eight or nine miles in the case of the Appian Way, the great south road from Rome — was lined with many handsome tombs and monuments. Nearly all of them are gone now; the famous round tomb of Caecilia Metella, its top sadly altered by battlements from its ancient shape, is the most perfect that remains; but in antiquity it stood in no such isolation, for it was only one among many family memorials.

Next, the traveller would reach the wall itself. City walls in antiquity were very high, and continued to be high until the days of gunpowder, before the advent of which the defenders feared not so much that walls would be battered down as that assailants would climb over them. The earliest city walls, like those of Roman camps, were earthworks; then huge blocks of stone were used, as in the Servian wall of Rome and in the walls of many other cities. A portion of the Servian wall, about forty feet in height, is still to be seen. Frequently there were towers along a wall, projecting forward from its general line, so that the defenders could assail the flanks of an attacking force with various kinds of missiles. Such towers appear to-day in the ancient wall of Pompei and in the Aurelian wall of Rome, though this was of course built much later than the period of which I am now writing. There would be a few gates in the wall, probably rather small if we may judge from the silence of Vitruvius, who says nothing about gates as ornamental structures, and from the only specimen remaining of the Servian gates of Rome. This gate is often unseen by travellers because it is built into a modern building, the Antonelli palace, where it forms the doorway to the principal staircase. The arched opening is not much more than six feet high, but the stones of which it is built are huge, some being five feet long. As time went on, however, the *Pax Romana* extended over the civilized parts of the world and city gates grew to be large, wide, and ornamental structures, such as, for instance, the Roman gate of Thessalonica, though they were still built thick and strong so as to withstand the possible attack of battering rams. It is not very easy for an American to imagine the appearance of a walled town, — either the look of the obstacle itself or the crowding of buildings and the narrowing of streets which were results of the limitation of space within it. We may get some idea of the conditions from old engravings of birdseye views of Rome and other cities, and we have on our continent at Quebec some remains of the old wall; but the first entirely walled city which an American is likely to see, is Chester in England. There one can walk all round the city on top of the wall, which stands much as it stood in the time of King Charles the First.

Having passed through the gates of an ancient city, most Americans (but perhaps not Bostonians) would be struck by the narrowness of the streets, just as people who come from the newer cities of the West are astonished at the narrow streets in the older parts of Boston. The streets themselves were well paved — and paved to last for centuries — with smooth blocks of lava or of the hardest stone that the neighboring quarries could supply. Earthen or gravel streets must have been rare in Roman cities. Often, as in many Roman and other Italian streets to-day, there was no sidewalk for pedestrians; but when there was a sidewalk, it was extremely narrow. Strangers think that the sidewalks in the shopping district of Boston are narrow enough, in all conscience; but they are broad compared to those

which we find in Pompei and in other excavated
ancient cities. Stepping stones were often provided at
the street corners on which to cross the pavement, when
it was being flushed with water to clean it or during a
rain. We still find such stepping stones in at least one
of our American cities, Baltimore. Very few trees were
to be seen in the narrow streets and only occasionally
a park, but there were many fountains; for the Roman
cities usually had excellent water supplies and the
climate led people to make great use of water. It was
brought from public reservoirs into the better class of
houses by a regular system of lead pipes, but the poor
went to the public fountains in the streets in order to
obtain it, as the poor in Italy do to-day. These public
fountains, running day and night, were provided in
great numbers throughout a Roman city, and from them
people who did not take city water by pipes into their
own houses could help themselves at will. When Agrippa,
the son-in-law of Augustus, was water commissioner
of Rome, he constructed for public use no less than
seven hundred basins into which water ran from below,
and five hundred fountains from which it spouted freely
into the air. That such fountains were in constant use
is proved by the well-known example in Pompei,
made of travertine, where the whole side of the cheek
of the little human head from the mouth of which the
water flowed, is worn away by the pressure of the myriad
faces which have leaned against it while drinking from

its stream. Many of the public fountains were decorative as well as useful objects, made of colored marbles or mosaics and adorned with statues. In some instances the water spouted from a shell or a vase or from the mouth of a bird; occasionally the fountain took the form of a niche, lined with mosaic work, a basin being placed below, into which the water poured from a jar held in the arms of a statue standing in the niche. Examples of all these and many other kinds of fountains have been discovered in Pompei.

Besides these fountains, great bathing establishments were also provided for the people, but these were of course under cover in buildings, and I am now sketching merely the out-of-door aspects of an ancient city. And so next must be mentioned the public squares or forums, originally intended for markets or political assemblies; but with the passing of popular government into the imperial system these spaces became the most ornamental parts of a city, surrounded with the finest temples and public buildings. We all, either from photographs or from an 'actual visit, know the Roman forum as a grand but 'pitiable ruin; ruinous, too, is the forum of Pompei, an array of broken columns with only the ground floors of the public buildings ranged behind them, and the great destroyer Vesuvius looming in the background over all. But in antiquity such public places were embellished with statues and other works of art — not rude and hideous objects, as are such things too often in our municipalities, but copies or adaptations of Greek masterpieces, or even those masterpieces themselves, brought by some Roman general or governor from Greek lands to adorn his native town. It is too much the fashion in our times to speak of the Romans as an inartistic people — a fashion perhaps led by the pretended contempt which Cicero, himself really an enthusiastic connoisseur, sometimes expressed when he wished to bring himself down to the level of an ignorant jury, or by the famous words of Virgil: "Others may mould the bronze to breathe more like nature, and may better hew the marble into forms that live, but, Roman, thou hast the ruling of men, — this shall be thy art, and to impose the habits of peace, to spare the vanquished and to trample on the proud." Perhaps indeed no real Roman ever became a great artist, but certainly the Romans as a people were great lovers of art and collectors of artistic work. Though they had no actual museums of fine arts and no permanent exhibitions in our sense of the word, yet many private houses were all but museums and, to a certain extent, were open to the public. Temporary exhibitions were held out of doors on the occasions of public festivals, and the official who presided over the festival would often borrow works of art from his friends to swell his own collection. Collections such as we find mentioned in Cicero's letters and in Pliny's *Natural History* are not made except in a country where there is real love of art. And we

find evidence of this love in small towns as well as in
Rome. It has been observed that the large number of
artistic objects found in little Pompei alone would
be perhaps impossible to parallel in any such small and
unimportant community at the present day. And when
we enter a modern gallery of antiquities, as for instance the Capitoline Museum in Rome, let us not forget how little we should know to-day about the history
of Greek art if it were not for Latin writers, or of the
actual appearance of Greek masterpieces if it were not
for Roman copyists and collectors.

Walking about in a Roman city one would pass under
numerous triumphal arches, stroll through colonnades
built for protection against the sun or for shelter in
rainy weather, note the shrines of divinities at corners
and elsewhere along the streets, and see certainly as
many temples as there are churches in a modern city.
One might pass a theatre or two, and perhaps an amphitheatre for gladiatorial shows or a circus for horse races,
though these latter buildings would probably lie outside
the city wall. Finally, one would observe that the
houses were built in blocks and were set flush with the
streets, that is, without intervening grass plots or veran-
das, and generally without flights of front steps, —
never with high flights of steps leading up to the doors,
as in some of our city blocks. Some few houses would
display columned vestibules, but these were the houses
of the great men of the city. The material of which the

houses were built was perhaps never wood, but either stone or concrete faced with brick, and the outer surface of the walls was usually covered with stucco. On the ground floor there were ordinarily no windows; Roman ideas of privacy within one's own walls forbade such openings. Sometimes the ground floor in the front part of the house was rented out for shops, as it so often is in the old Italian palaces to-day; in this case, the whole front of the shop lay open in the daytime and was closed by huge shutters at night. The principal street in Herculaneum, so far as that city has been excavated, and many of the Pompeian streets, afford us examples of such shops in the fore parts of private dwellings. If there were no shop on the ground floor, the wall would probably be blank except for the front door.   In the upper stories a few small and narrow windows might be seen, — mere slits for the admission of light and air; window glass did not begin to come into use until towards the end of the period which I have in mind. The real openings of the rooms of a Roman house were not upon the street, but upon the central court round which the house was built. Houses had usually two stories, and occasionally a balcony with small windows in it overhung the street. Every visitor to Pompei will recall the "house of the balcony" there. The elaborate frescoes discovered in a villa at Boscoreale on the slope of Vesuvius and now exhibited in the Metropolitan Museum in New York, show us houses with such balconies and apparently with more than two stories, but it is possible that the artist meant to represent several houses rising above one another on the side of a hill. We know, however, from Cicero and from Vitruvius that there were apartment or lodging houses of considerable height and many stories in the city of Rome; where the large population and the comparatively limited space made such devices necessary. And various laws to limit the height of these buildings were passed under the early emperors.

As one looked about him in the streets of a Roman city, undoubtedly the number of people visible there would be great. It is probable that no artery of trade in our largest cities is more crowded with people than were the streets of ancient Rome. This was because the Romans lived their life — even their private and social life — so much more out of doors than is the case in our country. To this day, the street in Rome called the Corso is spoken of as the only real club in town, and as many calls are paid at the doors of carriages on the Pincian Hill as at the doors of palaces beneath it. But in antiquity very few carriages or vehicles of any sort were to be seen in the daytime in the streets of a city. In Rome itself no private vehicles were allowed in the streets during the first ten hours of daylight. Almost the only vehicles permitted to use the streets by day were those which were driven in State processions or employed to carry material needed in the con-

struction of public buildings, or for other public purposes; private transport had to be done at night, and
of driving for pleasure there was none within city
walls. One might see highborn ladies or infirm old men
going about in litters borne by slaves, but as a rule
people walked; they had not lost the use of their legs,
they were not in the hurry in which we live, and they
had no problems of "rapid transit" to solve. The
streets, however, were crowded with people on foot,
engaged in the manifold occupations or pursuits of pleasure in which a Roman spent his day, and noise and confusion reigned in them. The shopkeepers and peddlers
were among the chief causes of the din. The former
pushed their counters, as the poet Martial complains,
far beyond the proper limits of their shops in order to
attract the attention of the passer-by, while the latter
cried their wares incessantly from sunrise until long
after darkness had come. There were the sausage men,
the cake sellers, the sweetmeat venders, the hawkers of
hot peasoup and cold fresh water, the old rags and rugs
and bedclothes men, the figman, the man who peddled
sulphur-tipped sticks as slowmatches, exchanging them
for broken glass, — all these and others of the same class
bawling their wares each in his own peculiar chant, the
actual words as unintelligible as are the words of our
old rag-and-bottle man to-day, but the intonation making the cry intelligible to the elect. Besides those who
carried their wares on their backs and the shopkeepers

who sold their goods over counters, there was a third class of dealers who set up tables temporarily here and there in convenient spots. Such, for instance, were the money changers, and the gold and bronze beaters of whom Martial speaks. These were like the men who sold and bought doves and changed money in the enclosure of the temple in Jerusalem, or like the retailers who are represented in a well-known series of pictures found in Pompei, which represent scenes in the forum of that little city. Here we see a baker, selling bread and cakes, dealers in pottery for household purposes, and ladies bargaining with other dealers for gowns. There sits an old fellow who has fallen asleep at his table, on which birds and fish seem to be exposed for sale; a gentleman behind him is poking him to wake him up to attend to customers. Next comes a man selling shoes to four ladies, one of whom carries her child. And farther on is a group of men who are perhaps taking their morning drink from a wine-seller. In Rome, many such dealers had stalls in the arches of the great Circus, or set up booths in open squares wherever their presence was tolerated. We can get a good idea of the character of such booths from details in the foreground of another well-known Pompeian picture, — that which represents the fatal riot which arose on one occasion during an exhibition in the amphitheatre of Pompei. This is but a rough sketch of the building itself with only hints of what took place, — mere samples of the crowd and the

surrounding objects, and so the booths in the foreground are doubtless only specimens of those which
filled the open space about the amphitheatre, like the
"sideshows" surrounding the tent of a modern circus.
We see two distinct types: a shed, and a much simpler
structure consisting of a huge square of cloth supported
at the four corners by poles. Such booths were not confined to the vicinity of amphitheatres, but were to be
seen throughout the streets of ancient Roman cities.
And in front of them, as well as in front of the more
permanent shops, another element of noise was to be
seen and heard, — a man employed like the modern
"barker" in front of cheap stores on the Bowery, to cry
the wares that were for sale and to lure customers to
enter and purchase. Such a man would pretty certainly
be employed by the jugglers and other vaudeville per-
formers who seem to have plied their trades in the streets,
at least in early days. Thus we are told that one of the
comedies of Terence was a failure because the audience
rushed out of the theatre to see a rope dancer in the
street. At a later time the jugglers, tightrope walkers,
tumblers, and balancers, often gave their exhibitions
in theatres or at private dinner-parties; but still there
were many who had no permanent place of business,
such as snake charmers, exhibitors of trained animals or
birds, and various sorts of athletes.

Beggars, also, swarmed in the streets of ancient cities,
just as until recently they swarmed in modern Rome.

The kind of beggar most frequently mentioned by the satiric poets is the whining victim of shipwreck, — Martial's *naufragus loquax*, — who carried about with him, in support of his claims, a bit of board on which the scene of the wreck was rudely painted. The same sort of emblem still survives with us in the pictures which we sometimes see on the top of wheezy little hand-organs, ground in our streets by self-styled victims of war or accident. The typical Roman beggar had a long beard, wore only a single garment, carried a staff, a scrip, and a scrap of matting on which to crouch, and was attended by a cross dog. His favorite haunts were the bridges, the city gates, the steps of public buildings, the forums, and the slopes of hills where people moved only slowly and were thus more exposed to his importunity. As the American traveller to-day whizzes in his motor-car up or down the hill between Albano and Ariccia, he passes unannoyed (but not uncursed) through the spot to which Juvenal alludes when he speaks of the "horrid blind flatterer that begs beside carriage wheels on the Ariccian hill and throws kisses after the carriage on its way down."

But we are getting outside of our city streets. Children abounded in them in the old days as now, playing their games with one another or tormenting the stranger. Here Horace saw a troop of urchins following and tormenting a half-crazy poet; there a gang of impudent street Arabs hustling a poor philosopher and pulling

his beard; there again a coin stuck fast to the ground,
with a group of grinning youngsters half-hidden somewhere near, hoping to see an unwary passer stoop and
try to pick it up — the same old trick that is still played
in modern times.

Among the more serious obstructions in the streets
were the numerous processions, which were often very
long and accompanied by a tremendous din from mu-
sical instruments, or by the shouts of frenzied worshippers or the screams of hired mourners. "These funerals
with their horns and trumpets meeting in the forum"
is Horace's notion of a great noise; it seems a strange
one to us who have come to associate silence with such
functions. Other processions were composed of fanatical priests, or generals in triumph, or trade guilds, like
the guild of carpenters which is marching in a Pompeian
painting. Then there was the long array of chariots,
horses, riders, and strange animals which passed through
the streets on days when shows were to be held in the
circus — the forebear of that which we still see when "the
circus" comes to town. An everyday sight was some
eminent man or popular politician parading down from
his house to the forum, attended by a train of supporters
and slaves which formed a little procession in itself,
with sneak thieves plying their trade among the crowd
that gathered as it went along. Towards nightfall one
might meet a merry wedding party escorting the bride on
foot to her new home, or a band of gay young fellows bent

upon a lark. Crowds were also attracted by the public
bulletin boards, the only means by which city ordinances
and notices of approaching public events could be dis-
seminated in the days before bell-ringers and printed
newspapers. A good example of the nature and situation of such bulletin boards is still to be seen to-day
in what is called the *album* at Pompei. Here, at the entrance of one of the streets leading out of the forum, was
a public building on the sides of which were twenty-six
blank panels set between columns, and on these panels
were discovered painted advertisements of public exhibitions, houses to let, sales, and other matters of common interest. In one of the Pompeian forum-scenes
which I have mentioned, we see men reading notices
on boards which ran from column to column of the
portico which surrounded the forums. These may have
contained edicts of magistrates and new laws.

Under such conditions with houses built in blocks,
and narrow streets filled with shops and thronging with
people of every sort, only the excellent system of sewers
and waterworks that prevailed in Roman cities pre-
vented an indecent and dangerous accumulation of filth
in the streets. The lower classes, however, were not
always scrupulous regarding the pollution of walls and
street corners, and appeals of various kinds had to be
made to them. Thus, one might see an inscription upon
a temple invoking curses upon the defilers of its walls,
and from such defilement, as well as from the scrawling

of trivial or obscene remarks, the usual method of escape was the painting of the familiar picture of the sacred snake, which made the spot where it was painted sacred to the genius or divine counterpart of it. As for the pavements, streets that sloped were often and easily flushed with water from the city pipes, but level streets or less important lanes frequently suffered from neglect, and the complaints of too much mud is a common one in the Latin authors. We are familiar with it in our own cities, and sometimes one feels tempted to try the Emperor Caligula's method with careless street commissioners. When Vespasian, who later became emperor himself, was only a street commissioner under the Emperor Caligula, the latter, on finding a quantity of mud in a side street, picked up a handful of it and threw it into Vespasian's lap as a reminder in kind of his neglect of duty.

The pushing crowds in the narrow streets must have been very distasteful to the higher classes of Romans, whose sense of personal dignity was always acute. In fact, allusions in Latin writers show that such personages considered themselves rather out of place there. They met each other rather in the great assembly-rooms of the baths, at temples, in libraries, in forums, or in porticoes. In the public porticoes, which often enclosed gardens, there was room for hundreds to walk in freedom from the confusion of the streets. Here were paintings, maps cut in stone, statues, beautiful shrubbery, shade from the sun in summer and protection from the wind in winter, cool fountains and fragrant flowers. In such places one would see more of the purple and crimson and brilliant white used in the clothing of the higher classes and of officialdom; but in the ordinary streets, color was as lacking as it is with us, — the dirty togas of the poor and the dingy or brownish cloaks and tunics of the working classes predominating there.

But what would be the appearance of the people themselves whom we should meet in a Roman city? Slaves of course would be there, brought from every outer nation and of every variety of mien and complexion. The citizens, however, would be more of one type, — spare and short, most of them, except in the north of Italy; for the average height of Romans was probably about five feet and five inches; — their hair black and crisp, usually merely combed forward over the head so that the forehead looked narrow; for a narrow forehead was to the Greeks and Romans a mark of beauty; — with their faces closely shaven during the whole of the period of which I am thinking, though in the earlier time they wore full beards. And so in the famous bronze head of Brutus, the expeller of the kings, we see him *barbatus*, "bearded." Of course this is not a contemporary portrait, for no such work could have been done in Rome when that Brutus was alive; but it was executed at least two centuries and a half before the Christian era, and it represented what people in those

days thought that this ancient Roman looked like. It
is an attempt to represent a definite individual, not a
conventionalized type; none of the sternness and
harshness associated in story with his character is
smoothed away; no unimpassioned blandness is foisted
upon this father of his country; he is distinctly ugly
even to his disproportionately large ears. And as one
examines other portraits of Romans, one sees that big
ears must have been a characteristic of the race. One
sees, also, how the individuality in these portraits
stamps them in their realism as something quite apart
from the work done by the Greeks, who do not seem to
have cared for realism in this department of art. But
to return to shaven faces: the earliest Roman of whom
it is recorded that he shaved every day was Scipio
Africanus, who flourished about two hundred years
before the birth of Christ. From that time and throughout the period of which I write, it was the Roman custom to wear no beard at all. The youth let the hair
grow on his face till his first shaving, which was a sort
of solemnity, the beard being cut off and dedicated to
some god. There was no special year for this formality.
Augustus postponed it until he was twenty-four years
of age, when he was already married and a member of
the Second Triumvirate. The famous bust in the Vatican, called "the Young Augustus," may therefore represent his appearance just after this time; for good
judges have remarked that this beautiful portrait has in

it little of the real freshness of youth; it is not Augustus
as a boy, if he ever was a real boy, but it shows how
early he began to do the work of a man in the world;
for he was only twenty when he joined Antony and
Lepidus in the Triumvirate, and therefore had not yet
begun to shave. Still, it is probable that the usual time
for the first shaving was between the ages of eighteen
and twenty, after which no Roman of standing wore
any hair on his face, except that young men of fashion
sometimes wore short whiskers on their cheeks. No
Roman ever wore the moustache alone; this was a
Celtic custom. Of course, however, we must remember
that the lower and poorer orders of the people were
not always able to follow the fashion of shaving; they
could not always afford to pay the barber, and so
Agrippa, son-in-law and minister of Augustus, when
he gave his first public spectacles, hired all the barbers
in Rome for the occasion to shave the poor, free of
charge, for several days. Hadrian, the first emperor
after our period ends, revived the custom of wearing
the beard, led to it, we are told, on account of scars upon
his face. The courtiers first and society afterwards naturally followed the emperor, and the full beard held sway
once more for nearly two centuries, until Constantine
the Great brought smooth faces into vogue again. Imperial fashions of this sort seem to have a strange attraction; thus, forty years ago the long waxed moustache and
"imperial" of Napoleon III led the fashion on the con-

tinent, and within recent times the upturned moustache
of the German Emperor finds many to imitate it. But
with us and in England to-day the smooth face is in
favor, especially with the younger generation; the
youth no longer yearns for a moustache, and to wear one
is coming to be the mark of an old-fashioned man. Such
details are not altogether trivial matters, undeserving
of the attention of the antiquarian; for a knowledge of
these fashions at different periods helps him in the identification of portraits which have come down from antiquity. And in other unexpected ways it may help
him. Thus, the modern investigators of the history of
horseshoes, who believed that a Roman relief at Avig-
non, representing a carriage and horses, was executed
in the time of Julius Caesar, did not know that the
bearded bust at the top of the monument (which he
omitted in publishing his sketch) showed that the work
was at least as late as the time of Hadrian. A gentleman with a beard would have been as surprising a phenomenon in Julius Caesar's day as in the day of George
Washington. The long procession which passed through
the streets of Rome on the occasion of the dedication of
the *Ara Pacis* by Augustus was composed of smooth-faced
men; not one of the many personages in it, whom we may
still see represented in the reliefs which adorned the
altar, has a beard or moustache.

But we must not be so ungallant as to forget the
women whom we should meet in the streets of a Roman

city, for the Roman women were not confined to their homes nor closely veiled in Oriental fashion when they walked abroad. They went out freely, those of the higher classes attended by one or more slaves; and frescoes show that they were as fond of shopping as are their sisters to-day. Their figures were often noble, and they had been taught in youth to move with grace and dignity; we should see, therefore, none of the tottering which is due to modern tight boots and high heels, or of that awkward dash, accompanied by masculine swinging of the arms which is affected by the present school of athletic women. We are all familiar, from works of art, with the simple, classic fashion of their dress; but we know also that all the fabrics of Italian, Greek, and Oriental looms were employed in it, and that in variety of colors, even in the streets by day, it could not be surpassed by any that we now see women wear at evening parties. In jewelry, too, nothing is produced by modern artists that exceeds in beauty or mere intrinsic value that which Roman women loved and wore. And no modern belle has greater skill in the more mysterious arts of the toilet, particularly in what concerns the "make-up" of the face. A whole street in Capua was given up to dealers who were as famous for their "beautifiers" as is any Parisian house of to-day. When out of doors, women generally drew a small covering over the top of the head, but not so as to hide the face or altogether to conceal the fashion in which the hair was dressed. The antiquarian or collector can no more afford to overlook changes of style in the hair of women than in the beard of men. Here, naturally, no one fashion lasted very long and there was a greater variety in fashions, but we hear nothing of "short-haired" women at any time among the Romans, nor do we see any such creatures in their works of art. And the diadem-like arrangement over the brow, called the *orbis*, was a wondrous structure, as little known under the Roman Republic or the first half-century of the Empire, as the "pompadour" and "rat" of to-day were known twenty years ago. The *orbis* is excellently represented on a gem containing a portrait of the daughter of the Emperor Titus, towards the end of our period. It is that "broidered hair" and that "outward adorning of plaiting of the hair" against which St. Paul and St. Peter, who saw the fashion coming in, warned the Christian women of their day.

But to go back into the reign of Augustus, the contemporary poet Ovid says that there were in his time as many ways in which ladies arranged their hair as there were acorns on the oak tree or bees on Mount Hybla. The whole passage in the third book of his *Art of Love* is worth reading, as showing how, in the opinion of this connoisseur, the hair should be dressed to suit the shape of the face, and not so as to follow any fashion blindly. Ovid, however, was writing for the gayer element in society, rather for those who depended upon personal adornment for their powers of attraction than upon rank and family. Women of rank, if we may judge from their portraits, dressed their hair simply in the times of the Republic and of the early emperors. Sometimes we see the hair parted in the middle, waving naturally at the sides, and gathered up into a short plait at the back of the head. Then a little later appears a "twist" of hair extending from the forehead back to the crown and thence down the back of the head to the nape of the neck, where there was a small knot. We have portraits of the Empress Livia, wife of Augustus, with her hair done in this fashion, and of Octavia, sister of Augustus and wife of Mark Antony, as well as of his earlier wife, the bloodthirsty Fulvia, whom perhaps we think of most often as responsible for the killing of Cicero. Gradually the arrangement became more and more artificial, with curls and ringlets in front and plaits behind, until it reaches the elaborate *orbis* which I have already described. Such a structure must have been exceedingly uncomfortable, but what will women not endure for fashion's sake? Almost as much as men, the discomfort of whose present costumes in our summers and "beaver" hats in winter has probably never been surpassed in the history of dress.

But to return to the faces which one might see in the streets of a Roman city, — among them might be those of the princes and princesses, of the great literary men, or of eminent statesmen and famous gen-

erals of those days, — of Caesar, for instance, whose
portrait upon a certain contemporary coin I confess I
prefer to any of the marble busts of him that are now extant. If there is anything in the study of physiognomy,
who would not prophesy victory to that strong, nervous
face when the man came into competition with Pompey,
— with Pompey as we know him now from the bust
in Copenhagen, and not from the Spada statue in Rome
which a mistaken tradition so long asserted to be that
at whose feet "great Caesar fell." But everybody knows
the features of men like these, for our museums abound
in casts and photographs of them; with the ordinary,
everyday citizens all are not so familiar, yet I admit
that I am interested at least as much in their portraiture as in that of the great men. For instance, in the
museum of Naples one sees Jucundus, the Pompeian;
the bronze bust of him, which once stood in his own house,
is one's ideal of the luxurious and prosperous broker and
small banker, and the account books found in his house
show that such indeed was his station in life. Near
Jucundus is another bronze head, thought to be that of
the Pompeian actor Norbanus Sorex, who also held
a municipal office; even without our knowledge that
tragedy was as dead in his day as in ours, we might
safely wager that his part was not "through pity and
fear to purge the soul of those emotions." And in
the Louvre is a nameless face, the detachable ornament
of a silver plate found among the Boscoreale treasure

just outside of Pompei, a bust less than four inches in height, but excellent in its details and obviously a portrait. One notes the wrenched features, the result, perhaps, of some disease, which produce the semblance of an everlasting mocking smile, the close cropped hair, and the huge ears which were typical of Romans. Then there is the old fellow who was found in the house at Boscoreale, lying not far from the treasure itself; perhaps he was the owner of it; but he is forever nameless, and what one sees now is only a cast made from the cavity left in the ashes where his body wasted away. In its poor remains, the head bears a curious resemblance to that of the street commissioner into whose lap Caligula threw the mud, and who himself became the Emperor Vespasian, — the honest and upright Sabine whose social reforms made as great a change for a time in court circles as was made in England by Queen Victoria and Prince Albert. The square-headed Vespasian reigned towards the end of our period. Going back into the time of the Republic, we find in the Vatican the portrait of one Septumius, — just who and what he was, we know not at all, but his portrait recalls all that we associate with the strenuousness, keenness and narrowness of a Cato or of a genuine New England Yankee of the old type. On the other hand, we have a unique terra cotta in the Boston Museum of Fine Arts than which, as regards mere workmanship, nothing better in the way of ancient portraiture is to be found any-

where in the world nor anything which can help us to
a better conception of the face of an enlightened Roman
of the higher classes in the Augustan age. Finally, a
tombstone in the Vatican exhibits a husband and wife
of the early imperial period. Helbig, one of the greatest
authorities on ancient art, believes that this work represents a typical Roman couple of the middle classes and
of native stock. The husband, he says, with his clear-
cut and wrinkled face looks like an industrious and pru-
dent head of a household; one would hardly ascribe
either poetic impulses or artistic tastes to such a man.
In contrast with his distinctly marked individuality,
the wife, who looks much younger, seems quite insignificant; one might guess that she was a virtuous wife
and a diligent housekeeper, but some would interpret
her expression as denoting shy reserve, others as down-
right dulness. Nobody, however, would fancy that she
was an entertaining woman, or likely to be stimulative
in her ideas. These two different characters in man and
wife, Helbig goes on to say, are not peculiar to this one
pair, but appear in many other nameless portraits of
the early Empire, so that it seems that the primitive
Roman characteristics often maintained themselves
in the middle classes in spite of all the influences of
Greek culture upon Rome.

Such, then, were some of the outer aspects of an
ancient Roman city, and such were some of the faces
that we might have met in its streets. Different in

many particulars from what is found in modern cities, yet in many others surprisingly like what one finds in them to-day, together they teach of the changes that come with advance in civilization and of the sameness which, in spite of what we call progress, is still to be observed in all that human beings do and suffer.

VI

PLATO AND PRAGMATISM

By CHARLES P. PARKER

PLATO AND PRAGMATISM

PLATO does not find favor with pragmatists. His genius they may admire; but the harm he has done to philosophic thought makes that genius simply baneful in their eyes. Just when the influence of Protagoras was guiding the young men of Hellas into science and humanism, just when the early investigators of scientific truth were finding in the martyred Protagoras a prophet, who inspired them to progressive study, and taught them to verify theories by human experience, — Plato's star appeared, and drew to itself the eyes and minds of men, away from the experience of life to an unreal region of thought. General ideas, the concepts formed by men to assist their inquiries, were canonized by Plato and were looked on as unchangeable truths. Meantime Protagoras, who always fashioned and freshened his thinking out of human life, had been misunderstood by contemporaries, driven from Athens, and drowned in the restless sea; and now, being misrepresented by Plato, when the world was just ready to understand him, was ruined as an influence for centuries. Plato thus appears to have been a fascinating leader of the unwary, drawing them by his magic music away from home-truths into mountains of perplexity and vicious intellectualism. Obviously a magician so potent as this deserves study, that we may learn the secret of his error, and save men at last from their long mistake.

The pragmatists have explained very clearly the nature of the mistake. They tell us that Plato supposes the concept to be itself the reality, and thinks that by handling concepts alone, without verifying and correcting them by constant reference to particular facts, we can attain truth. The right use of concepts, they say, is instrumental; their truth and value lie in their being instruments, by which we control the world and save ourselves from being lost in the rushing stream of our individual sensations. "Any idea," says Professor James, "upon which we can ride so to speak; any idea that will carry us prosperously from any one part of our experience to any other part, linking things satisfactorily, working securely, simplifying, saving labor, is true for just so much, true in so far forth, true instrumentally."

This instrumental view of an idea, as something on which we can ride, may oddly enough be very prettily paralleled and illustrated out of Plato's *Phaedo*. In that dialogue Simmias suggests that to know the clear truth about the soul is in this life something impossible or utterly difficult; but that if one cannot learn or discover the way of it he ought to take the best of human reasons, the hardest to refute, and riding on this as on an extemporized boat, sail through life at his own risk, unless one should be able to make the voyage by the

securer vehicle of a divine reason. And the illustration
is all the prettier, when one remembers how Plato uses
in this dialogue the word λόγος, here translated "reason."
He tells us that he was perplexed by looking at the
things, τὰ πράγματα (the pragmatist's world of experience), and therefore decided that he must take refuge
in reasons, looking in these reasons for the truth of
realities. Now to Plato reasons consist largely in the
handling of general concepts; and indeed in this immediate context of the *Phaedo* he proceeds to develop
some aspects of his doctrine of ideas. For this discussion he might seem to have prepared us in the earlier
words of Simmias, by the suggestion that reasoning
with general ideas may be a practical method of sail-
ing through the perplexities of life, saving us from death
by drowning in the swirling sea of sensations, even
though the idea may not be known to be eternally true.
Plato himself may perhaps think that he has found the
safe divine reason; but to us he seems to say, "Try my
ideas pragmatically, even if you cannot see your way to
accepting them as the ultimate truth. They will carry
you through the confusion of the world; they are at
least true in so far forth, true instrumentally." So
aptly does the illustration harmonize with our modern
pragmatic view that one might be tempted to suspect
that Plato had here utilized a passage out of the now
lost book of *Protagoras* on truth. In such a suspicion
we should simply, like other moderns, be building up

our view of Protagoras out of hints in Plato, aided by a cautious use of our own imagination. But at any rate Plato realizes that there may be human reasonings of great practical value, even when they are not absolutely coercive. He encourages us to search for such reasons; he warns us not to become misological when logic fails us, as men may become misanthropical when often betrayed by men. Thanking Plato then (or possibly his source Protagoras) for the excellent simile of riding in safety on an idea, the simile which Professor James afterwards thought out for himself and used so aptly in his own way, we feel drawn to explore the *Phaedo* and other dialogues a little further, that we may discover if possible the real danger of the restless sea of sensations from which both Plato and pragmatism, in unexpected temporary alliance, desire to save us.

In the *Phaedo* the difficulty seems to be bewilderment about causation. The experiences of the physical world come trooping along, pleasant and painful, beautiful and ugly, good and bad, great and little, single and double, hot and cold, odd and even, living and dead. They seem bound up together by strange laws of alternation; but the mind cannot conceive how in any way they cause each other, or how a world of such change and alternation can be caused at all. Yet we do at least find amid the confusion certain thoughts that are clearly distinguished from every other thought; each kind of thought is present from time to time in the pro-

cess of the world. Beauty, goodness, greatness, unity,
heat, life are ideas distinct from ugliness, badness,
littleness, duality, cold, death. We may say that a
thing is now hot and now cold, now good and now bad,
great in one way and little in another, two in one respect and one in another. But however the individual
things may change, the ideas are distinct, — and by
having the idea of heat in it a thing seems hot, by having the idea of greatness it seems great, by having the
idea of beauty it is beautiful. So too there are some
things that require a certain idea in them for their very
existence; a fire is not a fire without heat, seven is not
seven without unevenness, a soul is not a soul without
life. "Clear up your ideas," Plato seems to say to us,
"if you want to handle this perplexing world. Do not
say heat is cold, beauty is ugly, goodness is bad. The
world of sensations will drown you, if you cannot tell
one kind of experience from another, if you have no
general ideas."

Plato had tried to contemplate the processes of the
world directly, and had found them utterly bewildering.
"I became wearied out," he says, "in looking at reali-
ties ($\tau\grave{\alpha}$ $\check{o}\nu\tau\alpha$); and I thought I must take care not to
be dazzled and blinded by looking directly at the sun
of truth. I thought my soul might lose its sight by trying to use eyes and other organs of sense in gazing at
the things ($\tau\grave{\alpha}$ $\pi\rho\acute{\alpha}\gamma\mu\alpha\tau\alpha$). I judged that I must take refuge in rational thoughts ($\lambda\acute{o}\gamma o\iota$), and consider in them

the truth of realities." Ideas therefore were his refuge, his second best means of voyaging. The passage is thoroughly pragmatic. His ideas keep his thoughts clear, and enable him somehow to handle the world. In particular in this dialogue he comes through with the thought of the soul as a thing whose essence is life, a most practical thought which gives us the soul as the centre of our very being, and which sends us into life determined to keep this source and spring of all our life pure and free, a pragmatic belief which carries us into the world as conquerors, and changes the course of events. Protagoras himself could have asked nothing better and truer for the world. Plato almost seems to be under the influence of Protagoras, were it not that one element in the dialogue points in another direction. We must look sharply in this direction, to see if Plato's error may not be here. In the very passage in which Plato tells of his second best way of voyaging to seek the cause of the universe, in the very context where he says that he takes refuge in rational thoughts, and seems to imply that reasons are a mere reflection of reality, he adds: "Perhaps in one way my parable is unlike that of which it is a parable. I do not at all admit that a man who studies realities in rational thoughts sees them in an imaged likeness any more than he who studies them in the facts." The facts and works of the world, he seems to say, may be a mere reflection of realities as much as reasonings are. He even seems to suggest that the realities may prove to be rational. If such a doctrine be contrary to pragmatism, the line of divergence between Protagoras and Plato may be here. But one would hesitate to say that pragmatism denies the rationality of the universe; it merely puts us on our guard against thinking that our general ideas are the reality. They must be in some sense at least a mirrored image of reality when they guide us safely through the real world; and this is all that Plato claims for them. He does suggest that the working world of eyes and ears may also be a mere likeness of the real; but surely pragmatism does not insist on the valid truth of the sensational report. Schiller's Protagoras will not admit that, in saying "Man is the measure of all things," he means that truth is individual sensation. Of course such sensation is in one sense true; but objective truth is only that individual perception which has established its claim to validity by working. Let a man try to find his way through the world by trusting his immediate sensations without criticism, and he will come to grief. What Schiller distinguishes as claim and validity, Plato may intend by speaking of image and reality. There is a difference of tone somehow, but not enough to show a clear line of distinction between Plato and pragmatism. Surely this is puzzling and perplexing, that on our first approach to Plato we find such an appearance of partial agreement with Protagoras and Neo-Protagoreans. But Plato may have written the

Phaedo when partly under the influence of Protagoras and therefore unwilling to speak with too dogmatic a tone. We shall do wisely if we turn to another dialogue where the presence of such influence cannot be expected. Disconcerted by finding so modest and provisional a tone in the *Phaedo* we take in hand the *Republic*, hoping to find there a clearer line of demarcation from pragmatism. That difference of tone which we felt in the *Phaedo*, that greater trust in ideas than in sensations may take in the *Republic* more definite form, and reveal Plato's error.

But there is one characteristic of the *Republic* which we must notice before allowing ourselves to rely too much on any one section of it as Plato's final statement of truth. In it Plato the magician gives us a series of pictures which fade and vanish one into the other, each new picture retaining something of the old scene, but in such new connection that the whole effect is different. At any one stage you find the Platonic Socrates discussing quite seriously the commonwealth as if it were stable in its present form. But the city of cheerful animal-like men gathered round their perpetual picnic fire, baking great cakes, roasting their nuts at the fire, and drinking their wine, as they rest from their weaving and cobbling and farming, — soon changes under criticism into a city fevered with luxury, loving art, making war, and restlessly seeking happiness amid "diseases and accomplishments and sins." Soon

again, however, the luxurious city in developing its
trained warriors and equipping them for their work of
guarding the city, casts out as baneful all dissolute
art, even all unrestrained thinking, and finds itself
under the control of an educator who fills it with an
austere Doric beauty, making it a kind of glorified
Sparta. And this third city changes somehow into a
great communistic family where women are honored
and educated as no Greek city ever honored or educated
them, but where all the strength and charm of family
life as real men have known it is unsuccessfully merged
in a vain attempt to make all nobler citizens feel like
brothers and sisters to their equals in age, like children
to their elders. This communistic city in turn develops
a class of philosophers who color the whole picture with
a tone of high thinking and soon present to us a new
town, which depends wholly on the search for ideas and
the verification of them. Finally the external city,
failing to realize itself in this work-a-day world, is absorbed into the soul of the philosopher, and becomes a
spiritual city, an ideal in him and in us. With such a
shifting growing presentation of theories in this work
of Plato, we may not dare to detain our attention with
the theories of the fifth book on the nature of ideas.

In that book we do have the ideas presented as the
reality, the object of knowledge; while there is a world
of opinion which rolls between reality and unreality.
The particular things, which we suppose we see and

hear, at one time have a given idea in them, at another time have not. Shifting glimpses now of this real idea and now of that we do get. We are not mistaken when we feel that there is a kind of reality in the world of eyes and ears; but the real thought escapes the eye which tries to seize it, and a contrary thought appears in its place, itself soon to fade. All this line of thought is of course far enough away from Protagoras and his friends, who are constantly refreshing themselves from the world of sensation and testing their ideas thereby. In this book the idea does seem to be canonized and treated as the real permanent essence. But presto! change! behold in the sixth book these ideas as held by us and by most men are seen to be mere hypotheses which require verification. Indeed if one reflects upon the matter Plato seems in many dialogues to build up his general ideas out of the facts of this world with which our senses deal; and the general idea, suggested by the soul which looks at the world, is often tested by comparison with new facts and rejected because it does not explain them. Nothing is commoner in Plato than the rejection of one definition after another, and the ending of a talk with an unsatisfied longing for some rational account of a whole class of phenomena, such an account as shall explain and include them all; and the purpose of the search is practical, to wit, the guidance of life in days to come. It is the true Socratic method, gathering practical help out of the discussion as it runs through its imperfect definitions, but not attaining a permanent and unchanging truth. Even Schiller admits, under the influence of Stewart, that Plato may not be a complete intellectualist. But letting alone the Socratic dialogues, here in the *Republic*, in the stronghold of dogmatic treatment so-called, far away from the Socratic first book, the need of verification for our ideas is insisted upon. They are in themselves mere hypotheses. Whewell himself could not state the matter more clearly. Our understanding does indeed assume and handle the hypotheses with a feeling that it really knows them, but it gives to itself and to others no reason for the assumption. It treats them as self-evident, and proceeds with its demonstrations as if they were sure. It has a feeling that we cannot rise higher than these hypotheses; but this lower section of intellectual life seems to Plato's deeper thought unsatisfactory. No pragmatist could say more decidedly than he that we have no right to assume the universal validity of the concepts thus grasped by the help of sensation and unverified.

And the curious thing about Plato's proposed test of the truth of ideas is that he decides on their validity by examining the goodness of them. "If you can find what goodness is," *he seems to say*, "you will find that every true idea is a good one. Compare it with essential goodness, and if you can demonstrate it to be good you will see that it is thereby true. The presence of

goodness in the general thought is what makes it true."
This is not the method of a logician. One might almost
think that he was studying a modern pragmatist, except
for a transcendental flavor to the style in those passages
of Plato which *we* have reduced to commonplace.
But setting the transcendental flavor aside, what does
Plato really say and mean in the sixth book of the
Republic unless it be this, — that goodness is the cause,
the essence, the test of the validity of ideas? There is
no mere logic here. Plato is feeling his way out towards
truth, and is pervaded somehow by a conviction that
goodness is the final justification of everything. Reason
occupies itself, he claims, with seeing that things must
be true because they are good. Possibly the pragmatist
says rather that things shall be true because they are
good; but when he has declared they shall be, he goes
on to say that they are; and Plato when sure that a
thought is true in itself, proceeds to declare that in our
world it shall be. Here is at least some wonderful sympathy between Platonic and Protagorean thought.
The ultimate appeal to goodness is strong in each of
them. But what has the wizard Plato done with this
Protagorean doctrine, preventing the world from seeing
its real bearing, and substituting his own erroneous
point of view for the scientific attitude of Protagoras?
Perhaps his transcendental doctrine is the cause of the
mischief. He represents ideas as tested not by their
goodness in sensation and the world of sensation, but

by comparison with a mere thought of goodness, or by something which is higher than thought or reason, which refuses to play with sensations but will manifest itself only in general ideas as we compare them one with another. Plato thinks it hard to find reality in the flux and flow of sights and sounds, of tastes and smells and touches. James refers us to the flux and flow for our ultimate instruction. Plunge into the stream of life, the pragmatist says to us; there you will find real motion, sensations fading into sensations, life burning and changing, progressing with vital energy, flinging itself with creative power into new and ever new forms. Thought cannot detain or limit it. Conceptual thinking is merely a way of trying to handle it. Live and you shall really know. Thuswise the pragmatist; but what says Plato? Rise above the changing sensations into thoughts that are clear; rise above your own thoughts, for they are inadequate, rise into a world of essential goodness and beauty, where the sunlight of goodness pervades the bright universe, causing and revealing thoughts beyond all your present thinking, overflowing with its radiance even into the world of eyes and ears, giving to sights and sounds and fragrances such reality and beauty as they can catch in their passing.

One must say that here by either path, following James or Plato, one comes into a mystical region, where rational thinking seems to fail us, where life is given as the cause and ground of knowledge. Dive into the stream of life, says one; fly into the heaven of life says the other. In either case you plunge or you soar (what difference is there anyway between up and down for a metaphysician?) into a region of mystical reality where reason cannot fully follow, but which vivifies reason, and which reason tries to describe. In either case it seems to you splendid and refreshing, and you try to get other people to dive or fly with you; and you do make the venture seem attractive, though you find it hard to say clearly just why. Is it not possible that Plato and James mean the same thing approached from different points of view? A turbid wild thing the world seems to some; to Plato its ultimate reality seems beautiful and full of peace and a great calm. Are we quite clear in our minds that reality must be essentially restless? Suppose I take the pragmatist-Heraclitean metaphor, and say that when I plunge into the river of life, it takes me up in its great peaceful arms, and bears me along, strongly, quietly, while the trees of life grow on either side of the river, and birds of heavenly beauty sing glad songs to the rising sun. Am I then no longer a pragmatist? The question is a vital one. Does pragmatism always lead to turmoil, or may it lead to peace? Does Plato's error lie in his deep persuasion that the essence of life is peaceful and permanent, that goodness when attained is quiet and restful as well as strong? Pragmatism ought to mean a certain openness of mind; pragmatism ought to use general

ideas as helps to life rather than as masters of life; pragmatism ought to be always testing its ideas by the value
of them as working instruments of life, that is by the
goodness of them; pragmatism ought to be progressive;
but pragmatism can hardly deny an instrumental value
to ideas which set the soul at peace. If all this is true,
Plato begins to look like one of the princes of pragmatism.

But the impression must be one of Plato's magic illusions, to the end that, by seeming to agree with Protagoras in many ways, he may entice the pragmatically
minded to leave the great teacher of humanism, and may
at last undermine their principles. Pragmatism is, as
has been said, progressive; it is a movement, not a
frozen dogma; and Plato puts no trust in motion.

He may not trust motion, but he seems to love it.
Full of variety, warmth, and life are the quick-moving
thoughts of the dialogues, by which he tries to suggest
to us what he conceives reality to be. They are a very
inartistic background for his thought if they are par-
ables of a real world which is supposed to be frozen
forever in mere sculptural and architectural beauty.
But Plato's world of reality is no mere abstraction from
earth; it is a great idea shining in what he calls "the
multitudinous sea of beauty," which a true lover of
wisdom learns to contemplate. Sparkling with the energy
of some eternal motion the universe must be. Plato
approaches its essence in the *Phaedo* through the idea

of life, in the *Republic* and *Timaeus* through the motion
of stars, in the *Symposium* and *Phaedrus* through the
idea of love; — a love which in the *Phaedrus* is mad-
dening, bewildering, full of intense activity. A reality
which is approached through thoughts of star motion,
life, love, and radiant beauty cannot be conceived as
a dead thing. And indeed Plato tells us himself clearly
in the *Republic* that there is real motion. "The bright
manifold beauties of the sky," he says, "in the visible
world, must be considered as the most beautiful and
exact of all visible things; but we must believe that they
fall far short of the true movements ($\phi o\rho\acute{a}s$) wherewith
real swiftness ($\tau\grave{o}$ $\grave{o}\nu$ $\tau\acute{a}\chi os$) and real slowness ($\acute{\eta}$ $o\mathring{v}\sigma a$
$\beta\rho a\delta\acute{v}\tau\eta s$) move in real number and in all true forms,
relatively to one another, carrying with them all that
they contain. Those movements are to be grasped by
reason and understanding, not by sight. We must use
the bright manifold beauties of the sky as though they
were diagrams drawn by an ancient artist of heroic
days, just as a geometrician uses his figures, to lead to
thought." Clearly true motion is to Plato's mind an
element of thought; the pragmatist cannot claim a
monopoly of it if he expels Plato from partnership with
pragmatism. And indeed in the *Sophist*, that great
dialogue in which Plato clearly prepares the way for the
more fully developed metaphysics of the *Timaeus*, Plato
arguing with Eleatic logic overturns some of the great
dogmas of Eleaticism and shows motion, as he shows also

otherness, to be essential parts of the universe. One
can see the deep feeling wherewith he almost pragmatically insists that logic shall give us a world of life and
activity. "Ah, Zeus! Shall we really ever persuade ourselves easily that motion, and life, and soul, and thought
are not present with absolute being, that it does not
live nor think, but stands solemn and sacred, without
thought, immovable? That would be a terrible piece
of reasoning to admit. Are we to say it has thought,
but not life? Are we to say that thought and life are in
it, but that it has them not in soul? In what other
manner could it have them? Shall we say it has thought
and life and soul but stands altogether unmoved, with
a soul in it? All this seems to me irrational. We must
admit that motion and the thing moved are realities."
Plato will believe in motion. But what is true motion,
in his view? What is its relation to those bewildering
movements in space, which seem to confuse his mind,
which even a modern pragmatism with difficulty can
explain?

The relation of any idea to space is a puzzling thing.
In the dialogue *Parmenides* we can see clearly that the
criticism of Plato's doctrine of ideas is made from the
point of view of one who cannot conceive of anything
except as extended in space. Indeed one suspects that
the notion of space is an axiom of the Eleatic philosophy,
and that we must conceive of the great Unity of *Parmenides* as A. W. Benn thinks of it in his book, *The*

Philosophy of Greece, "as something like the dreamy
space enclosed between that unislanded sea and that
unclouded sky on which the low-lying shore of Elea's
neighbour Paestum still looks out." Nearly all Greek
philosophers, except perhaps Pythagoreans, seem to take
space for granted as a prerequisite or a part of the essence of being. At any rate in that vivid dialogue in
which Plato admits and emphasizes the criticisms
made upon his doctrine of ideas, the thought of space
is implied and is used to overthrow the ideas. "If the
whole idea is in each particular thing of its kind, then
it will be separate from itself"; as if it would lie extended
in space with each particular thing that shared its nature. "If it covers a multitude of particulars it will
touch each of them with a part of it, like a sail spread
over a number of men." "If the particular thing has
in it only a part of the idea, then the idea is divided;
can it be one?" "If you cut off a part of the idea of
greatness and put it in a particular thing, can the part
of greatness, being less than greatness, make the particular thing great?" "If you take a part of the idea
of littleness, and add it to a particular thing, will not
even the tiniest bit of littleness make the thing greater
than it was before?" "If you say that the idea of greatness makes a thing great, is not the idea itself simply
another great thing alongside of the other particular
great things?" All through the discussion, wherever
the young Socrates tries to suggest that the idea is a

thought, or anything like a thought, the veteran Parmenides takes it and spreads it out in space, and makes
it look ridiculous. But Plato felt that he could not give
up his belief in the ideas, for they seemed necessary
to clearness of thought, in fact to any thought and philosophic discussion at all. As a result probably of the
criticisms on the doctrine, admitted in the *Parmenides*
to have a certain force, Plato decided at last that space
is an illegitimate product of reason which darkens the
understanding of an idea. The *Timaeus* contains his
solution. All this world with which our senses deal pre-
supposes the notion of space or place. Space is cut up
into tiny geometrical forms in which ideas are present
somehow, but so that they easily vanish and give place
to others. In this world of space the confused illusive
motions glimpsed by sensation take place. But what
is the cause of this confused and changing space-world?
Plato has a suggestion to make. The suggestion, if we
may venture to interpret it, in our own words, out of the
Timaeus, seems to be this: God is good, and an essential
characteristic of goodness is that one cannot be satisfied with being good, but must give goodness and happiness to others. Therefore God has in his essential
thought the idea of souls of lower gods (like Hebrew
angels), of men and of animals; and his goodness must
overflow in and into these souls, creating a universe
full of his goodness. But the very idea of a soul, especially of a human soul, is of a being which has spatial

relations, which provides itself with a body, which sees and hears events as if they were in space. Thus the soul must try to figure ideas to itself in space; but the divine ideas cannot be limited to space or understood in space, which is an illegitimate offspring of reason; the soul therefore becomes perplexed and cannot be happy. Now let us add the *Phaedrus* to the *Timaeus*. The soul, deep sunken in the spatial changing world, catches a gleam of the divine beauty of the ideas, even in those faint fleeting glimpses of them which its eyes see in space and its ears hear. This is the divine attraction, drawing the soul away from the imperfect space revelation back to the source of all goodness and happiness. Helped by a friend, or better still by a city of friends, it turns away from merely spatial things and rises to the heaven of ideas as the gods see them. So the divine motion works in a circuit through the life and love and social activity of souls, putting souls forth, and drawing souls back to itself, in a divine circuit of intense activity and varied beauty, which is faintly imaged by the revolutions of stars in the visible sky, and of which the shifting, changing, perplexing world of space gives only a troubled dream.

Surely Plato believes in motion. But one says, this is very transcendental. Yes. But does pragmatism forbid one to hold a transcendentalism which works, which changes actual life, which makes the world different? "Ah! but," you say, "Plato is so dogmatic and so sure!"

Not at all. He distinctly says in the *Timaeus*, "If we
give reasons as probable as any, we must be content,
remembering that I who speak and you who criticise
have human nature; so that it becomes us to accept the
probable account of those things, and not to seek anything further." The *Timaeus* is thoroughly modest and
pragmatic; unless pragmatism always insists that we
shall approach reality by the path of sensation. Do you
answer that Protagoras would never have travelled by
Plato's visionary path? Visions like Plato's can change
life. True, you reply, but Protagoras would have promoted a movement like our modern science; and Plato
killed the movement by his distrust of sensation, and
by his insistence on his doctrine of ideas.

Pragmatism, then, must be scientific; that is the
position. And Plato is not scientific; that is the error.
At last we are tracking the wizard to his innermost
castle and home. So with redoubled attention we give
our minds to the state of science in Plato's time. The
Greek philosophers had grasped the idea of the three
states of matter, solid, liquid and gaseous, and of their
changes into one another. They called them, it is true,
earth, water and air, but the essential notion was the
modern one. If they added to these a fourth state of
matter, fire, this was not unlike the modern speculations
which resolve all matter ultimately into electric units.
They had also some idea of the relations of heavenly
bodies to one another and to earth, and began to have

some understanding of eclipses, with some power to
predict them. The apparent celestial sphere with its
zones and the ecliptic were understood; possibly even
the spherical shape of sun and earth, and the zones of
earth. Thus elementary astronomy was developed as
well as elementary physics. Physiology also had received much attention; the processes of nature were carefully observed and ways of assisting nature to heal were
studied. Some idea even of the relation of the brain
to thought had been gained, and at least some elementary suspicions as to the nervous system in connection
with sensation. Guesses had been made about atoms
which curiously anticipated modern doctrines of mole-
cules. Anaximander had perhaps guessed at the development of man from animals. Empedocles may have
guessed the survival of the fittest. Xenophanes had
argued that mountains and islands were once under
the sea, arguing from sea-shells and fossils found there.
Many guesses less successful had been made about light-
ning and earthquakes by reasoning from analogy.
Many queer ideas about stars had been broached by men
in the infancy of scientific investigation. But the
principle of watching nature had been introduced; and
men had learned to infer what will be from what is and
has been. There was a real beginning of physiology,
physics and astronomy; there was also some elementary
study of problems in logic and psychology, in ethics and
politics, though the study of rhetoric had a tendency
to overshadow them.

But the solemn truth is that these scientific activities were far removed from modern sciences of the same subject-matter. They had much acute observation; they had clever hypotheses; but they lacked verification, they needed more careful classification, they lacked precision and exactness. Physiology would seem to have been as careful as any, as able to predict the future, as capable to anticipate and prevent. But in astronomy, meteorology and physics there were wild desultory guesses; in ethics and politics and psychology there was a surface study of conditions but no penetration to the depths of the matter. More observation was needed, more classification, less vague generalizing, less following of surface analogies, and always careful measurement. Into this world of crude science Protagoras had come with his famous aphorism "Man is the measure of all things, of realities that they are, of unrealities that they are not." Obviously he was in sympathy with all movements which encouraged individual human activity; certainly he must have valued individual sensations and perceptions; clearly his philosophy might have worked well with the observations of Ionic physical philosophers or with the atomic theories of Leucippus, destined to be developed by Democritus, the townsman of Protagoras; nor would the developments of medical study as they came along have been out of harmony with his principles. Moreover to the theories of the time he might have contributed a valuable criterion of truth. "Take careful note of what you perceive," he might have said; "the sights seen by your eyes, the sounds heard by your ears have great truth and value. Build your theories first on what you see and hear and touch; but remember that the senses of other men, if they are as careful as yourself, have equal value with your own. Your theories therefore should be built not only on your own experience, but on that of other men. Remember also that they will build theories as naturally as you. Man is the measure of all things, but it takes all of us to make Man. The teaching of a whole city has more value than that of any one citizen, unless the citizen has taken unusual means to inform himself. A leading professor of wisdom, for instance, may have a better truth than that which other men have; and the test and proof of the greater excellence of his truth is that it works good results. Working power is the best proof of the validity of a theory. Good truths, which work well for men, get combined in a body of truth which we may recognize as valid and objective." A movement of philosophy and science, based on such principles as these, Protagoras might have started. There seems to be no proof that he began to do so; but to do it would have been in harmony with his known lines of thought as they are indicated, though perhaps half concealed, in Plato's *Protagoras* and *Theaetetus*. And even if Protagoras himself had not gone so far, some disciple of genius, some ancient Schiller, might have arisen to consecrate the master's memory in Protagorean dialogues and to develop his humanism and scientific interest along these lines. Under such influence the atomism of Democritus might have found a freer, more humanistic development than afterwards the dogmatic Epicurus and his school gave it. Under such a teacher the impulse to research in a mind like that of Aristotle might have taken a direction more like modern science, and shown results even more striking than those which interest us much later in the Roman Lucretius.

But how would classification and measurement have fared at the hands of such a Protagorean school? Socrates was the man who realized the importance of having a clear idea as to kinds of things. Plato, following Socrates, was the man who dwelt on classification, and said to the world, "Clear up the meaning of your general concepts." By such attention to general ideas his thoughts were indeed drawn away from trust in particular sensations. These shifted and changed so quickly that when he had caught a general idea from them he easily let them fly away. But the general ideas which he loved are of the utmost importance for practical guidance in this world. Doubtless he exaggerated their value, and perhaps pragmatic methods would have prospered better if some man of less genius than Plato had undertaken to develop the teaching of Socrates, and had kept general concepts within more modest limits, allowing more for the value of sensations. But even as things stood Aristotle did qualify the doctrine of ideas immensely by respect for individual observations. Therefore Plato, followed as he was by Aristotle, may be said to have contributed to science the idea of classification without really overmuch transcendentalism. Certainly in and after Aristotle's time the Greeks went on with what we call their scientific study. Plato does not seem to have killed it entirely.

But though science went on, perhaps pragmatism did not. The Greeks were still vague and speculative; and the guilt of this is laid at the door of Plato. "Man is the measure of all things," said Protagoras; but Plato had somehow discredited both Protagoras and Man. What Plato objected to, even in such a high-minded professor as the great teacher from Abdera, is not very difficult to see. He feared that human opinion would be made the standard of truth; even in that attractive picture which he draws of him, in the dialogue called by his name, he makes Protagoras undertake to show that Society teaches political science. Plato himself thought that we must find some better teacher, if our beliefs are to be surely good. But this reference to a better standard than Man is what seems to trouble the modern pragmatists. Their idea is that before the better standard can be made effective Man must grasp it; and they believe that Protagoras would have interpreted his measuring Man as including far-sighted prophets who see workable valid truths before the multitude grasps them.

Truly a beautiful vague phrase is that "measure of all things." What does it mean? It might mean almost anything. The great need of Greek science in the days of Protagoras was the application of exact measurement to phenomena. We may imagine that he hinted at this, if we like. But there seems not a shred of evidence that he cared about having instruments of precision, or about applying mathematics in scientific inquiry. Schiller suggests that when Protagoras had said "Man is the measure of all things" the next natural question was "Then how do we manage to measure?" Any thorough answer to this question would include the statement, "Man measures phenomena by mathematics." Plato has twice thrown before us in his dialogues the thought of the importance of the measuring art. Once in the *Protagoras* he dwells on it, inspired perhaps by the famous aphorism of the great Sophist with whom he is dealing. He shows that to find our way safely through the world we need to measure things and find their true relative value. This is a thoroughly pragmatic position. Again in the *Politicus* he explains how important in art work of all kinds, with a view to finding the true proportion of every element, is the measuring art. These hints might well have led to showing the importance of precise measuring instruments, if Plato had cared to dwell more steadily on the world of material things. But at any rate he did more than most men of his time to encourage mathematical study of all kinds. The value of mathematics and the interest of the work is one of the thoughts most markedly found in Plato. Arithmetic, plane geometry, solid geometry, the mathematics of star motion, the mathematical theory of music, — all these studies he urged in his *Republic*. The Greeks studied such subjects for the absolute interest of them, and so handed on to the world the instrument which later scientific men have used to measure realities. The scientific speculators of ancient times did not see their way to a wide application of mathematics except in astronomy and music. Perhaps they loved their vague guesses at truth, and their qualitative observations. Perhaps they did not care to measure except in art work. Perhaps it simply never occurred to them to do so much measuring of shifting phenomena. Yet to develop the sciences which measure was a good practical piece of work, even though they knew it not. Plato might seem to have done no mean service to science, not only by promoting classification but by encouraging the study of mathematics. If he had been caught young by Protagoras instead of by Socrates, and had been turned into an advocate of pragmatism, he might have seen more clearly the value of individual perceptions, and might have been drawn by his natural tendencies to combine with their study some application of mathematics. Yet if Plato had died young, and had been no man's disciple, we may well doubt whether any one else would have arisen with genius sufficient to impress the world in this way. Regretting, if we choose to do so, that he followed Socrates rather than Protagoras, we shall perhaps, as things are, do better to give him credit for what he has done for science, rather than blame him for preventing the growth of a somewhat shadowy earlier pragmatism. Perhaps a real pragmatic movement could not have flourished except as a protest against the over-dogmatism of the human mind. At any rate there does seem rather imaginative evidence that the philosophy of Protagoras would have developed into an anticipation of the movement of Schiller, Dewey, and James.

Meantime Plato has been shown to have advanced his views with much modesty, and not to have claimed that he personally had made the absolute verification whose need he felt so deeply. And his school after him, when a brief period of dogmatism had gone by, became for two centuries a centre of open-minded inquiry, whose aim was to discredit dogmatism, and itself to find the best and most probable good counsel for practical life. The spirit of Plato, the lover of an unattained wisdom, the seeker for practical good, was surely alive in the New Academy. This New Academy throws a curious light on the claim that Plato loved dogmatic philosophy, and killed free scientific inquiry. The progress of mathematics, and researches such as those of Archimedes, throw another curious light on the claim that Greek science was killed at all.

And so where have we arrived in our inquiry ? We were grieved to find that Plato had checked and killed the growth of an early Greek pragmatism; and we determined to find the secret of his error. We thought we should find it in his view of the general concept as a fixed and final reality ; but we soon saw that he used his concepts instrumentally like a good pragmatist. We thought the deception might be found in his transcendental endeavour to fly higher than thought; but we soon saw that pragmatists would dive out of thought into the stream of life, and we perceived that mysticism was not contrary to pragmatism. We thought it unpragmatic to talk of testing ideas by the presence of the idea of goodness in them; but immediately this appeared to be simply a queer way of declaring the essentially pragmatic doctrine that the test of the truth of an idea is its value. We thought that Plato's endeavor to escape from the turbid stream of life was an unpragmatic endeavor to avoid the living fiery creative reality; but we hesitated to commit pragmatism to saying that the reality of life could not be a heavenly peace. We thought that Plato's distrust of motion must be the centre of his error; but we have heard him say himself that he does not believe in an immovable world, that motion has in it the essence of being. We thought that the real trouble must lie in Plato's dogmatism; but we have found him modest and provisional in his philosophy, and the animating spirit of the open-minded New Academy. We thought that the difficulty lay in his unscientific attitude; but we found that he gave to science classification, and did all in his power to urge men to the study of mathematics, without which modern science could never have done its work.

The greatest difference between Plato and pragmatists all through the inquiry has seemed to be, on his part, a certain distrust of sensation. It is true that Plato loves to use his eyes, and that his eager spirit searches out the immediate facts of the Greek world and sets them before us in living colors. It is true that he claims for the fleeting impressions of the moment a presence of eternal realities which in that swift passing they reveal; he does not deny all reality to sensations. But he does distrust the world of eyes and ears and touch; he finds no rest for himself on the tossing changing sea of phenomena. Pragmatism seems at home on the sea, and does not distrust sensation. Whatever other likeness to pragmatism Plato may show, he cannot simulate this. He has taken refuge from our search in one disguise after another, as believing in the instrumental character of concepts, as testing the truth of ideas ultimately by their goodness, as being modest and open-minded, as loving scientific inquiry. Unless there is something else than all this in pragmatism, we shall find difficulty in expelling him from our company, and in aiming rightly our blows against his philosophy. But there is one disguise impossible for him. If an essential part of the method of pragmatism is to treat sensations as the great reality, and to find matter more solid than thought, Plato stands revealed as the enemy of the pragmatic movement; we have tracked the wizard to his last hiding-place, and know where to strike if we wish to destroy his power.

VII

OVID AND THE SPIRIT OF METAMORPHOSIS

By EDWARD KENNARD RAND

OVID AND THE SPIRIT OF
METAMORPHOSIS

HAD Mr. Palgrave compiled an anthology of Latin
verse besides that treasury of gold for which every
lover of English poetry is thankful, he would have
found no place in it for Ovid. In his admirable little
volume on *Landscape from Homer to Tennyson*, he dis-
poses of Ovid as "amongst world famous poets, perhaps the least true to the soul of poetry," and finds
the *Metamorphoses* "of all over-praised poems, over-
praised the most." Ovid has been little read since the
Romantic invasion, and is hardly more than the shadow
of a name, though not a great name, to the general
reader of to-day; in any five-foot compendium of universal culture, few would spare Ovid an inch. And yet,
after a somewhat chequered career in the late Empire
and early Middle Ages, Ovid became, from the eleventh
century on, one of the absolute and indispensable poets.
He fascinated not only the mediaeval imagination, but
also, perhaps even in greater measure, the Renaissance,
with its homesickness for antiquity. No fame seemed
more secure than his, and nothing occurred to damage
it, until Romanticism came. A poet who influenced —
I am thinking not of arrays of parallel passages, but
of the penetrating effect of temperament on tempera-

ment — a poet who profoundly influenced Chaucer, Spenser, Shakespeare, deserves consideration at least from the chronicler of literary developments, and even, it may be, has something of immediate value for our own generation.

Nor has Ovid been utterly without witnesses during the past century. Not to dwell on various appreciative observations in the volumes of Sellar and Mackail, Landor declared for Ovid in no uncertain tones. In one of his imaginary conversations, he makes Messala remark to Tibullus:

In every department of eloquence and particularly in poetry, we look for depth and clearness; a clearness that shows the depths; here [in Ovid] we find it.

Perhaps we should not hold Landor responsible for an opinion dramatically assigned to someone else, — indeed he has given us warning on that point, — but in another of the conversations it is Landor himself who says to the Abbé Delille:

Virgil is not so vigorous as Lucretius, so elegant and graceful as Catullus, so imaginative and diversified as Ovid. All their powers united could not have composed the *Aeneid*, but in the *Aeneid* there is nothing so epic as the contest of Ulysses and Ajax in the *Metamorphoses*. This in my opinion is the most wonderful thing in the whole range of Latin poetry, for it unites (what appears incompatible) two pieces of pleading never excelled by Roman or Athenian orator, with exquisitely discriminated characters and unparalleled heroic composition. The *Iliad* itself has nothing in the *contentional* so interesting and so animated.

This is rather extraordinary from Landor, who was not given to exaggerating Roman excellence at the expense of the Greeks; on the contrary, he was somewhat fond of showing the Romans their place. His criticism here may not be particularly nice — few would select "deep" and "epic" as appropriate epithets for Ovid — but one may appeal to the passage as a counter-blast to Palgrave.

What are the abiding qualities in Ovid's greatest work, his *Metamorphoses?* I believe it his greatest, though remembering how Macaulay regarded the *Art of Love*. The school-boy to-day, sometimes his teacher, too, thinks of the *Metamorphoses* as primarily a store-house of the myths in which Greeks and Romans believed; he reads from selections which give no idea of the whole. True, the poem has always had a subsidiary use ever since the days of the later Roman Empire, when for pedagogical purposes it was turned into prose. It is a serviceable guide to the illustrious fables of antiquity, which some of us still consider an essential part of a liberal education; moreover, it has been a Bible of Poets, and, in the Renaissance, a Bible of Painters as well. But if Ovid suspected that we saw in his work a *summa mythologica*, he would turn as uncomfortably in his grave as when the mediaeval pilgrims said prayers there, in the hope of his conversion, and heard a voice in answer:

Nolo pater noster;
Carpe, viator, iter.[1]

If we would reach the inmost meaning of the *Meta-morphoses*, we should first follow the clue given in Ovid's previous works and his career. I can do no more in the present paper than make this approach. Of Ovid's career, we have information vouchsafed by himself. One of his poems of exile, the poem which he perhaps thought would be his last, is a brief autobiography. He tells us there of his early inclination to poetry, and the vain endeavor of his father, an honest merchant of the equestrian order, to start him on a political career and the pursuit of the *denarius*. While a member of one of the inferior courts, the young man spent less time with his colleagues than with the poets about town; the latter he calls gods on earth. Poetry came so easily to him that it was actually a bother when he attempted commonplace prose:

Et quod temptabam dicere, versus erat.[2]

The opposite experience, alas, is more common. Ovid, with Pope and Lamartine,

"Lisped in numbers for the numbers came."

Among the men of letters with whom Ovid was familiar were Propertius, Ponticus, Bassus. He knew

[1] "No Paternosters, I pray;
Traveller, go on your way."
[2] "And what in prose I tried to say, proved verse."

Horace and heard him read his poems; he pays Horace the compliment of not infrequent imitation in his own poetry, and Horace returned that kind of compliment in the opening poem of his final volume of lyrics — the reason why we shall see later. Virgil, Ovid "only saw." Tibullus, too, had died before he could claim real friendship with him, a fact that he deeply regretted, since Tibullus was the master of both Propertius and himself. For the first poems of Ovid of which he gives us definite information were love-elegies in honor of the imaginary Corinna:

> " When to the world my earliest songs I gave,
>   My cheeks had known their first or second shave.
>   Ambition stirred me when the whole town rang
>   With that feign'd name Corinna, whom I sang."

It was a time of romantic *Sturm und Drang* with Ovid, if we may take him at his word:

> "Soft was my heart, for Cupid's shaft fair prey,
>   Ever to trivial impulse giving way.
>   Though such was I, kindled by slightest flame,
>   No tale of scandal ever breathed my name."

My subject does not call for further reference to Ovid's autobiography, entertaining though it is. I wish only to make clear Ovid's interest in his earliest poetry, his love-poetry. He calls himself in the opening verse

> tenerorum lusor Amorum [1]

and he does not refer to the *Metamorphoses*. This is

---

[1] "Playful singer of the gentle loves."

no sign that he thought the later poem an inferior affair; simply, his immediate purpose calls for no mention of it. He is writing, at what he thinks the end of his career, not merely an autobiography, but, in a way, an *apologia pro vita sua*. He does not, in the fashion of his previous letter to the Emperor, which forms the second book of the *Tristia*, seek to palliate each detail or enlarge on his later and more sober poetry; on the contrary, he singles out for reminiscence his earlier work, the cause of his disgrace. There is something of a challenge in the title "playful singer of the gentle loves," as though he preferred that to any other. The phrase and the cadence of the line take us back to the opening verse of the last poem of the *Amores*,[1] and though he doubtless has in mind his love-poetry in general, he thus emphasizes his earliest work. Unlike many another poet, Ovid did not regard his youthful verse as futile; all the more reason for turning first to that, in our endeavor to apprehend the secret of the *Metamorphoses*. Though by no means his greatest achievement, the *Amores* is immensely significant and typical; it contains the elements of all his later interests.

The love-elegy had already had a history at Rome before Ovid turned to it; in fact, if a recent theory is true, we may accredit the Romans with the invention of the personal elegy, a type not developed by the Greeks. Ovid mentions himself as fourth in the line

[1] Quaere novum vatem tenerorum mater Amorum.

of succession, Gallus, Tibullus, and Propertius having preceded him. Catullus, too, cannot be neglected, for the full comprehension of the matter; he is not mentioned by Ovid, because according to the rules of ancient literary criticism he is strictly not a writer of elegy at all. Including him, as the modern reader must, we see the more clearly a development, or rather retrogradation, in the elegy, from intensely real and personal feeling to the artificial, the imaginary, the didactic. Tibullus and Propertius were in love with real beings, but the mistresses of their poems were often the mere personifications of traditional devices and situations. For Ovid, if we accept a too prevalent opinion, there was nothing left but to make his love entirely fictitious and spice his episodes with pruriency. Conventionalized lewdness is the sum and substance of the *Amores*, according to a recent German critic. But here we wonder what Horace saw in these poems to call forth from him his notable tribute of imitation, and if we turn to the eleventh of Horace's epodes, we shall discover why.

> "I care not now, oh Pettius, as of yore,
> Verselets to write when Love is smiting sore,
> Love, that selects me most of all the age
> For tender boys and tender girls to rage.
> Thrice has December laid the forests bare
> Since for Inachia I've ceased to care.
> 'T is mortifying, now, to write me down
> An ass, dear me! the fable of the town.
> How I detest these banquets to recall

When the fond lover was exposed to all,
By speechlessness and stupor now depressed,
Now blowing sighs out from his inmost chest.
'Aye, think of it! The poor man's brilliant wit
To cope with gold is utterly unfit,'
I'd moan to thee, when the immodest bowl
Opened at last the secrets of my soul.
'Had I a spark of righteous indignation
In this poor breast, I'd tear off my vexation, —
This poultice of false shame that heals no sore —
And free, I'd wage the unequal fight no more.'
When so I spake, severe in virtue's praise,
Told to go home, I'd totter by strange ways
To hostile doors, alas, thresholds of stone,
That racked my legs and loins in every bone.
And now a lad, who boasts himself the peer
Of any little luscious damsel here,
The lad Lyciscus has made slave of me,
From whom nor kind advice of friends can free
Nor pointed insult, but some fresh affair,
Radiant girl or slim boy debonair
Tossing from out its knot his flowing hair."

How much of this poem reflects Horace's personal experience it were hazardous to state; very little, I fancy. What most forcibly impresses the reader is the quiet satire at the expense of the lover, whose rôle the poet assumes here and in various of his odes; in one, in particular, we find him singing what the ancients called a "closed-door serenade," out in the rain, on the uncomfortable sill. Now the overwhelming grief of love and the consequent inability to versify, a gloomy demeanor at banquets, despite of the wealthy and successful lover, appeals before the cruel portal — these are moods and episodes treated with all seriousness in the elegy of Tibullus and Propertius. Horace's love-poetry is not all satire; far from it. But its delicate and delightful quality is due mainly to his irresistible sense of humor, which plays on the surface of sometimes deep emotion, dispelling the mists of the morbid and sentimental. Did he invent his device of gently laughing at the third person in the guise of the first? It is at any rate an admirably protective and effective device.

Now Ovid took this hint from Horace, and developed it into a system; we may note, in passing, that the first poem in the *Amores* contains an obvious reminiscence of the eleventh epode. Ovid speaks in the *Tristia*, we have seen, of his tender and vulnerable heart, but, truly, it was a heart encased in triple brass. The lines are about as applicable to Ovid as the eleventh epode is to Horace. Incidentally it is worth observing that the solemn protestation in the *Tristia*

nomine sub nostro fabula nulla fuit [1]

is flatly contradicted by one of the *Amores*. In that poem he tells of bystanders pointing him out — as Dante was pointed out in the streets of Florence, for a different reason — and exclaiming

hic, hic est, quem ferus urit Amor.[2]

---

[1] "No tale of scandal ever breathed my name."
[2] "There, there's the man whom mad love burns."

Then he adds the reflection

Fabula, nec sentis, tota iactaris in Urbe.[1]

Now is not this melting swain, the slave of ruthless Love and the talk of the town, is he not the same ridiculous character that Horace for the same purpose chose to assume? *Fabula quanta fui!* Proceeding in this spirit, Ovid elaborates the woes of this poor lover with all possible detail. He, like Horace, attempts a closed-door serenade.

> "Porter, fast-bound — what outrage! — with hard chain,
> Fling wide the unrelenting door again!
> I ask but little, and if that won't do,
> Open half way; I'll squeeze in side-end to.
> Long love has thinned my body purposely;
> Subtracting flesh, it adds agility.
> Love steals me gently past the wakeful guard;
> I cannot stumble, though the way be hard.
> I used to dread grim phantoms of the night,
> And wondered who dared roam without a light.
> Laughed Love, a laugh Love's gentle mother gave
> And lightly said — I heard them! — 'He'll be brave.'
> Love came a-sudden: I have no dismay
> For flying shades of night or traps by day.
> You, torpid one, I fear; you I cajole,
> You have a thunderbolt to blast my soul.
> Look — drop the bar, 't is easier so to peep —
> Look at the sill all dripping where I weep.
> When once you stripped in terror for the blow
> 'T was I, faith, begged your mistress grace to show.
> What, shall the gift that your salvation brought —
> Oh infamy! — avail the giver naught?
> Show gratitude; you'll find it not in vain.

---

[1] "Thou art the talk of town, and knowest it not."

Night's hours fly; oh slip the bolt again!
Come, slip it back. Then live from fetters free,
Nor taste for aye the cup of slavery.
You hear, hard heart, while vainly I implore,
Yet bars of oak still hold the rigid door.
'T is well to man the walls in war's alarms
And bar the gates, but why in peace fear arms?
How shut you foemen out, if so the swain?
Night's hours fly; oh slip the bolt again!
I come escorted by no arméd band,
I was alone, were Cupid not at hand.
Not though I wished it could I banish him;
Easier were to tear me limb from limb.
Love, then, and on my brows a dash of wine,
And wreath from wet locks slipping — these are mine.
Such harmless weapons who would not disdain?
Night's hours fly; oh slip the bolt again!
Art numb? Or stands Sleep — curse you! — at your ear
This lover's words into the wind to veer?
Once I recall, when *out* I sought to glide,
Till midnight's star you waited, open-eyed.
Perchance your love is sleeping with you now;
Better to you than me the fates allow.
Were such my luck, I'd don your iron chain.
Night's hours fly; oh slip the bolt again!
Can I be wrong, or did the hinges creak?
I judge the door is moving, by that squeak.
I'm wrong. A puff of wind, in straying by
Rattled the door — and blew my hopes on high."

So much of the poem will suffice to show Ovid's intention. Can we imagine that he takes seriously the woes of this flouted gallant and the anti-climax of his disappointment after the smooth Tibullan serenade with its ludicrously formal strophes and refrain? A lover who has time to observe in his shrunken body the workings of the Darwinian law of natural selection is not suffering from a broken heart; we doubt if he has lost much flesh. Ovid delights in exposing him to embarrassing and ridiculous situations. I will not stop for other illustrations from the *Amores*, but add merely that the fair maiden is not infrequently served the same treatment. In brief, Horace is Ovid's master and model in this new species of elegy, far more so than are the elegiac poets themselves. To appreciate the *Amores*, read Horace for its animating spirit; for the sources of its originality read Tibullus, though he deals with the same material, for contrast, not comparison. If ever the gentle Tibullus is humorous, it is from no fault of intent.

I am far from meaning that the only interest in the *Amores* is the amusing parody of what Ovid's predecessors in elegy had treated seriously; Ovid also takes a genuine delight in intrigue as a fine art. It is absurd, however, to call the *Amores* or the *Art of Love* sensual — "the most frankly sensual poems ever written." With his incorrigible sense of the ludicrous, Ovid is at times indecent to the point of blasphemy, but he is not filthy like Swift or prurient like Sterne; and he was no more affected by any of the "perturbations" than is the Stoic sage. His supreme quality is wit, as Shakespeare saw; Ovid calls his muse *genialis*. It is not sensuality but mental audacity that leads him to treat with an exuberance of detail and an evident relish of the task, matters that Horace would not have touched. What Horace was delighted to see in Ovid was exactly the same attitude to romantic elegy that he had; this accounts amply for the compliment that he paid the younger poet, and we need not inquire what he thought of other elements in the *Amores*, or what he would have thought of the *Art of Love*. Tibullus, in that imaginary conversation of Landor's, remarks: "Before I left Ovidius he read to me the commencement of some amatory pieces, at which, if I smiled, it was in courtesy, not approbation." There is another cause from which he might have smiled, namely, a sense of humor.

A recent German critic does not smile for any reason; he scowls and sighs, missing the lyric impulse in the *Amores*, "das Herzens auf- und abwogende Stimmungen." But in like manner one might be dissatisfied with Rabelais for his noticeable lack of religious emotion. Ovid must be judged by the standards he professes, and really he is writing not lyric, but partly dramatic, partly expository or didactic poetry. The tendency to didactic had become prominent in Tibullus and in Propertius, as Ovid, anticipating modern critics, pointed out; for in apologizing to Augustus for his *Art of Love*, he cites the authority of Propertius's "enticing precepts."[1] Now it is this very element that Ovid himself exalted into the guiding motive of his elegy. There is no fundamental difference between the *Amores* and the *Art of*

[1] Invenies eadem blandi praecepta Properti.

Love; in fact, as every reader knows, there are striking coincidences in episodes and details. The *Amores* is nearer to the drama, giving in its separate elegies little episodes of comedy, like the mime, but it is no nearer to lyric. That Ovid felt the kinship between his two works is shown by his use of the same metre for both. Starting as an ostensible follower of Tibullus, he wrote short poems in elegiac metre, startlingly different in spirit and mainly didactic in contents. Planning a new work, one entirely didactic, a mock-didactic, he adhered to the metre of the *Amores* because the undertaking was essentially the same; this was decidedly an innovation, as didactic poems of the type which Ovid was following normally required the hexameter. Now the *Art of Love*, though one of the supreme parodies in all literature, may be criticized for various defects, of which a breach of courtesy against good taste is one; Landor's remark, "from the mysteries of religion the veil is seldom to be drawn, from the mysteries of love never," contains deep truth. But not even the German critic in question would censure the *Art of Love* for lacking the lyric impulse.

After thus finding wit a dominant element in Ovid's temperament, wit irrepressible, ready for display at most inappropriate times and places, we may next examine a matter important for the understanding of the *Metamorphoses*, namely, the glimpses of mythology that appear in the *Amores*, and the spirit in which Ovid treats

it. In one of the poems, which presents another of
those unfortunate situations that true love confronts
in Ovid's elegies, a lover makes a passionate appeal to
a plebeian little brook, which, thanks to a freshet, has
suddenly swollen to a river and is interrupting the
lover's morning call. The latter, after much suppli-
cation, wishes that he had the wings of Perseus or the
self-impelling car of Triptolemus, adding immediately,
however,

> "I prate of ancient poetry's monstrous lies
> Ne'er seen or now or then by human eyes."

Sentiment like this from the author of the Bible of
Myths is at first sight surprising. Ovid treats the gods,
moreover, most cavalierly, for instance in a discourse
on their grossly partial treatment of maiden's oaths:

> "Believe that gods exist! She broke her vow;
> Her face, though, beauteous then, is beauteous now."

As with Horace's maid of Barium, perjury brings no
penalty to fair woman. With mere man, the poet
finds, it is different:

> "By her own eyes my darling lately swore,
> And then by mine; and mine are aching sore!"

He therefore proposes the irreverent dilemma:

> "Either gods are mere names, an empty fear,
> And stupid crowds believe whate'er they hear,
> Or if a god there be, the amorous thrall
> Lets pretty damsels lord it over all."

Yes, over gods as well as men. Men serve as targets for
the martial deities, but

> "Offended gods fair women fear to offend,"

as the poet proves by various "olde ensaumples" of
divine amours. And yet, with a generous burst of compassion,

> "But why reproach high heaven, why scandals tell?
> Have not gods eyes, have not gods hearts as well?
> Were I a god, I'd see no damage came
> To pretty maid foreswearing by my name.
> Yes, I'd swear maids swear truth at any odds!
> You would not class *me* with the gloomy gods.
> But thou, fair damsel, use the great god's prize
> More moderately; or spare, at least, mine eyes."

Ovid's aptitude for treating the gods as lightly as
he does the lover does not speak for much interest in
mythology on his part. Yet he is powerfully fascinated
by myth-making of a certain kind. In the poem that
contains his first declaration of imaginary love, the oath
of eternal fidelity to Corinna, he remarks, after ringing
the changes on this note:

> "Oh give me for my song a joyous theme.
> And worthy of its source, songs forth shall stream.
> To song the hornèd Io owes her name,
> And she to whom the River-bird brought shame,
> And she who by the Bull o'er ocean borne
> With maiden hand held tight the crumpled horn.
> So we alike shall make the whole town ring;
> My name to thine conjoined all time shall sing."

Here is mythology in which Ovid can believe — the
immortality which the bard and the bard alone can

give to great men and deeds, an idea that Theocritus and Horace had set forth finely. Ovid goes farther; he takes pleasure in assisting at the process of immortalization. He gives his Corinna — need we say she is a fictitious being? — the reality of Io, Leda, Europa; and they are as real as she. Here is at once a thoroughgoing scepticism as to the truth of ancient myths, and a lively faith in the creative imagination.

Then Ovid proceeds to play with this idea, as he plays with most ideas. In a subsequent poem, he laments that he himself is responsible for Corinna's infidelity, not only because he had given her complete instruction in the art of love, but because by his clever portraiture he had invested her with a fatal charm. The Muses, he cries, should have shown him less favor, Phoebus should have left him in the lurch.

> "Now courts accept not poet's evidence;
> I would my words were credited less sense."

Poets are responsible for such legends as those of Scylla, Perseus, Enceladus, the Sirens; he names a dozen others, including several metamorphoses in the list of poetical transgressions:

> "Thus runs on poets' license without end.
> Nor doth historic truth their words attend.
> You should have known my love was praised by me
> Falsely; I'm lost through your credulity."

So, besides wit, an essential quality in Ovid's temperament is the joy in creating myth, in proving unrealities real. In this art, few poets are more imaginative than Ovid, though his imagination often descends to what Wordsworth would call fancy. Without a trace of romantic wistfulness, without a sigh over the present, which he adores, he delights to project himself into the unknown and build his habitation there. This power, that he shared with Goethe,

"in der grossen Welt eine kleine zu machen,"

served him in good stead during his exile, a tolerably unpleasant experience, which he took not too seriously, rather, perhaps, not seriously enough. In one of his poems of exile he pictures himself at Rome with his friend Macer, and then by the magic of fancy summons Macer to his side. Likewise in his brief autobiography he declares:

> "In that I live, then, and these hardships fight
> Nor am aweary of the daily light
> Thanks, Muse, to thee! Thou solace dost supply,
> Thou rest from cares, thou balm for misery.
> I call thee, guide and mate, and Gothland 's gone;
> Thou givest me abode on Helicon."

With Ovid as with Milton, the mind is its own place.

Wit, the faculty of mythologizing, of building an imaginary world — these are traits that are obvious in Ovid's earliest and latest works. Another which immediately concerns us, on which, in fact, I would make the present discussion converge, is his fondness for the metamorphosis. I mean not merely the metamorphosis of legend, but the idea itself; Ovid delights in his own power mythologically to transform as well as mythologically to create. Nothing pleases him so much as suddenly to shift his point of view, and after declaring his allegiance to one aspect of a situation, immediately to present the exact reverse with an equally convincing sobriety. We have seen his first declaration of love, in which he pledges loyalty to a single mistress. Following farther the series of his imaginary experiences, we turn with something of a shock to a poem which describes his embarrassment at having two sweethearts at the same time. He consoles himself with the reflection:

"Better to have double love, than never love at all."

And what shall we say of that humiliating confession of his, in which he explains with exuberant detail just why he has to love every maiden that he sees? Similarly, in one poem, the lover gives elaborate instruction to his mistress how to deceive her husband at a banquet to which all three are invited; in another, he describes his bitter pangs at finding that she has applied the lesson to deceiving her lover instead. Now the identical material of the latter poem we have in an elegy of Tibullus, and a comparison is instructive. Tibullus's woe is genuine, relieved only by one of his rare flashes of unintentional humor; as an instance of his sufferings for his mistress, he recalls the time when he was chased all night by her dog. Ovid takes as much relish in describing how his mistress deceives him as in formulating a

code of deception for her use in his favor. The details
are exactly the same as in his previous poem; he likes
to manipulate and readjust them. He is not absolutely
angry at his love when he can stop to set forth in an
elaborate series of similes, the different blushes which
his reproofs evoke; he is not so indignant at finding that
with a new master she has made even further progress
in the art of love, as he is interested in making this
observation. Again, as we have seen, he first exalts his
creative power which places Corinna among the mythologically famous, but later, he laments that his art has
been taken seriously; the rôle of *sartor resartus* Ovid
immensely enjoys. To continue these illustrations, we
find in one poem an entreaty to a husband to guard his
wife well, that Ovid may find the intrigue exciting. It
is possible that this is ironic advice, given to an ultra-
cautious husband, in the hope that he will overreach
himself by guarding his wife less closely and thus give
the gallant the chance for which he is waiting. However
this may be, equally earnest counsel is elsewhere given
the husband, *not* to watch her too strictly.

I will not follow further the workings of this spirit of
metamorphosis in the *Amores*, but will turn for a moment to the *Art of Love* and the *Remedies*. In these
poems, which should be considered as forming a whole,
we have a veritable triumph of wit. In the main plan,
they form a mock-didactic; the title *ars amatoria* is
meant to suggest the *ars grammatica, ars rhetorica*, that

the schoolboy knew. We cannot translate this title
Manual of Love, but *Art of Love* is just as one-sided;
Ovid's contemporaries knew the double meaning of the
word.   I must repeat my opinion that there is no pruriency in the poem. Its eminent qualities are audacity
and satire; the satire on the Tibullan elegy that we
have seen in the *Amores* is universalized here. The
poem is also a triumph of the metamorphosis, satirical
metamorphosis, at the expense of the lover and the
poet. Books I and II of the *Art of Love* form a learned
manual for the lover, whereby he can overcome the
wiles of his enemy — *fallite fallentes*. This much formed
a little work by itself, circulated about for a short time,
and then Ovid, undergoing a metamorphosis, came out
with Book III, a manual for mistresses, with exactly
the same purpose as the first instalment — *fallite fallentes*. To these distressing text-books he finally, in
response to his critics, added the *Remedies* as an ironical *apologia*, turning the tables on both the preceding
works. This palinode is likewise a satire on his critics.
Instead of humbly repenting, as they desired, and instead of pointing out what a ludicrous figure he has
made of the lover, he falls back on the argument from
authority and the appropriateness of his material to
his theme. He left it for those who could detect his
satire to find, as Dryden found in the fourth book of
Lucretius, that ridicule is a most potent remedy of
love. But the Puritans of Ovid's day drew one false

conclusion from his works, and the entourage of Julia drew another.

To appreciate in a striking detail what I have said of this general spirit of metamorphosis in the *Art* and *Remedies of Love*, consider the counsel given the lover courteously to apply to faults the names of contiguous virtues and thus enjoy them as such. Plato, Lucretius and Horace had preceded Ovid with similar remarks; his words have the tinge of parody of a well-known theme.

> "Names can tone ugliness; call her brunette
> Though her complexion be as black as jet.
> She squints? So Venus. Glares? Minerva's look.
> 'Lithe' let her be, if skinnier than a spook.
> Call puny, 'trim'; for turgid, 'buxom' say,
> And thus with bordering good, defects allay."

This is from the *Art of Love*. In the *Remedies*, naturally, the prescription is reversed, Ovid first applying the cure, in an extravagant form, to himself.

> "'How lean my darling's ankle!' I would say;
> And yet, truth tell, 't was not at all that way.
> 'My darling's arm, how ugly!' Truth to tell,
> My darling's arm became her very well.
> 'How puny!' She was not. 'What bills she sends!'
> Ah, that is why my love in rancour ends."

Then, speaking generally, and treating the words of his former counsel to a kaleidoscopic change:

> "'Turgid' the buxom, 'black' the brunette call,
> And swear the lithe lass has no flesh at all.
> If she's not rustic, call her saucy-faced;
> And 'rustic' call her, if perchance she's chaste."

Really, the nimble Ovid is turning so many metamorphoses, that were the last verse quoted apart, even an
expert would imagine it came from the *Art of Love*, not
from the *Remedies* of the same.

Ovid's most obvious gift, conspicuous even in selections from the *Metamorphoses*, is his narrative facility;
this trait of his, doubtless, was a formative influence on
two admirers of his, equally great *raconteurs*, Chaucer
and Boccaccio. And though the situation might not
demand it, the call to narrative was heard, and answered,
even in his earliest work. There are more chances,
naturally, in the *Art of Love*, and the narratives there,
such as the story of the rape of the Sabines, show greatly
increased powers. But even in the *Amores* glimpses
appear, in particular the legend of Ilia, with which
the thwarted lover regales the insolent brook; for the
moment, the reader forgets the setting of the story,
lost, as its author lost himself, in the sheer exuberance
of narrating.

For once, therefore, we have caught the audacious
teacher of amorosity in a serious mood, or something
that approaches it. We should remember, likewise,
that while writing *Amores*, he was planning a tragedy.
In the first poem of Book III there is a debate, suggest-
ing somewhat the allegorical *conflictus* of the Middle
Ages, between Elegy and Tragedy. The palm of victory is given temporarily to the former, but in the last
poem of the book, the customary metamorphosis

occurs; it is now farewell to the loves, and welcome the new and more venturesome emprise. Moreover, for another sign that Ovid was not giving his entire attention to his little world of satire and intrigue, we may turn to the thirteenth poem of the same book. This is a description of a festival of Juno at Falerii — this and nothing more. The revelation of Ovid as a sober family-man going some distance through a hilly country with his wife to attend a religious ceremony is startling at first, but not when we know our poet better. The rites are described with patent sincerity and interest; indeed a Roman poet cannot go for long without displaying the national passion for liturgy. The idea of including a poem like this in the *Amores* may well have been suggested by the archaic and national pieces in the later books of Propertius, which are recognized by everybody as precursor of the *Fasti*, but it has a higher value in unmasking the real character of the poet of the *Amores* for the benefit of those who take some of these poems too literally. While, once more, I should be the first to admit that Ovid can let his wit run too far — *nimium amator ingenii sui* says the wise Quintilian of him — and that he descended to most questionable taste and something worse, still, a reading of the *Amores* can hurt nobody with a sense of humor, and as those without this sense will find the poems dull, they too will be immune.

Nor has Ovid failed to make a similar revelation of

seriousness in his *Art of Love*. Toward the end of Book III, the story of Cephalus and Procris, a story of pure conjugal affection, which he repeats in the *Metamorphoses* with touches of genuine tragedy, shows the reader that background of feeling and character without which satire becomes both harsh and ineffective. This is his real "apology" for the *Art of Love* — not the so-called *Remedies*. This is why the story is set conspicuously at the close of the earlier poem; Ovid had anticipated his Puritan critics. But he was too subtle to reply in exactly the language which they demanded. If they could not taste the fine flavor of his wit, that was their look-out, not his.

The preceding argument has shown, I hope, that the *Amores*, apart from its own merit, is biographically significant in that it presents in the germ all the vital interests to which Ovid later turned. Though his nature was subtle and complex, its development was beautifully simple; like Plato's metaphysics according to Schleiermacher, or Christian theology according to Newman, it was all present at the beginning of the course. One mood only, the product of externals, of an unkindly blow of fate, does not appear — the mood that found expression in *Tristia*. This aside, we can see why Ovid was temperamentally impelled to metamorphoses for a subject.

It is interesting to know that Ovid heard the elder Macer read from his poem of metamorphosis, the *Orni-*

thogonia; it is well to gather what we can of parallels between Ovid's poem and various works of the Alexandrines; and even, if truth really demands it, we must accept the unpleasant hypothesis that he drew from no more sparkling a source than a mythological handbook. The quest of models and influences is valid and important, provided the seeker knows the real object of his search; an unfortunate delusion, however, has too often appeared in our generation, the delusion that if the poet has by his magic converted dross into gold, the careful analysis of the pedant can prove the gold mere dross after all. Pope knew the process, but little guessed the triumphant minuteness with which critics of our day can humble the strains of ancient poets:

> Turn what they will to verse, their toil is vain,
> Critics like me shall make it prose again.

It is only when the study of the sources of a great poet discovers the secret of his originality that it deserves encouragement, since it immediately involves the analysis of the poetic temperament. That is the quest to which the critic first should turn; for the poet's chief sources are himself and the Muse.

In brief, then, as we have found, Ovid was first and last fascinated with the world of mythology, which stretches into the beginning of time but is accessible to the present as well, a free country, wherein the creative imagination can roam, forming and transforming to suit its pleasure. Ovid was interested in causes, in the process of making the irrational plausible. The theological doctrine of *creatio ex nihilo* would have given him no difficulty, for the reason that his is a most startlingly monistic universe; all miracles are fictitious, but all are natural and real. His power to tell of what he fancied, apparent in his earliest work, increased with practice; an easy plausibleness is its distinguishing virtue, which sometimes slips into the contiguous device of artificial dexterity. Turning to the historic and pre-historic past, away from Corinna and the world he had built about her, he is involved necessarily in matters more solemn than the art of love; his own nature, too, as even the *Amores* tells us, was imbued with the Roman love of liturgy and tradition. But there is no cleavage of his life into halves, as with Boccaccio. A comparison of the *Amores* and the *Amorosa Visione*, the *Metamorphoses* and the *De Genealogia Deorum* is tempting, but appears ridiculous the moment it is made. Ovid's life is of one piece. His earlier work leads naturally to the later; in a word, the reason why he devoted a long poem to metamorphoses was not because any number of pre-decessors had done the same thing, and not because he saw the utility of a Bible of Myths, but because his temperament felt most at home in a world of meta-morphosis. Change and transformation in the realm of ancient legend allured him now, because in that little world of contemporary mythology which he had built, change and transformation had played a sovereign part.

My paper must end here; it has pointed the approach but refrains from entering that pleasant country which Ovid discloses for us in his greatest poem. But to confirm the preceding analysis, I must briefly refer to the most important passage in the poem, the most important, that is, in the way of formal declaration of what is implicit in every line; I mean the description of Pythagoreanism in the last book. In following the course of metamorphoses from "Nature's birth to Caesar's times," Ovid has come to the reign of the good king Numa, and accepting the dubious tradition that Numa acquired some of his lore from Pythagoras, expounds, in part, the latter's supposed tenets. This is essentially germane to his plan; he selects that one of the little systems of philosophers which insists most clearly on the process of transformation which he has been tracing in all history human and divine. We cannot safely assume such Pythagoreanism as Ovid's own belief, any more than we can assume as Virgil's own belief the lofty metaphysics which makes possible the vision of Roman history in the sixth *Aeneid;* in either case the doctrine is explained by the dramatic necessities of the poem. But in either case, the doctrine is an index to the poet's temperament, setting that forth with something of the directness of dogma. Ovid declares his allegiance to a universe of flux and flow, which he has been describing in every conceivable way. Lucretius, though not blind to the impressiveness of change, depended for his soul's serenity upon the vision of atoms indivisible and indestructible, which guaranteed the permanence of things. Ovid could complacently remark, and thereby anticipate the conclusions of our New Physics:

Haec quoque non perstant quae nos elementa vocamus.[1]

The whole passage is notable for its imaginative brilliance and its sombre, almost mediaeval mood of reflectiveness, in which, however, no touch of romantic yearning is appreciable. Not in vain did Shakespeare remember the lines in one of his best-known Sonnets:

"Like as the waves make towards the pebbled shore
   So do our minutes hasten to their end;
   Each changing place with that which goes before,
   In sequent toil all forwards do contend."

He must have known the following verses from the *Metamorphoses*. I give them in the version of Golding, which Shakespeare knew, as well as in the original, which he knew also.

Things eb and flow, and every shape is made too passe away.
The tyme itself continually is fleeting like a brooke,
For neyther brooke nor lyghtsome time can tarrye still. But looke
As every wave dryves other foorth, and that that commes behynd
Bothe thrusteth and is thrust itself, even so the tymes by kynd
Doo fly and follow bothe at once, and evermore renew.

   Cuncta fluunt, omnisque vagans formatur imago.
   Ipsa quoque assiduo labuntur tempora motu;
   Non secus ac flumen; neque enim consistere flumen

---

[1] "These, too, last not, which we call elements."

Nec levis hora potest; sed ut unda impellitur unda
Urgueturque eadem veniens urguetque priorem,
Tempora sic fugiunt pariter, pariterque sequuntur.

Cuncta fluunt; πάντα ῥεῖ. A world of flux and flow,
but the victorious imagination its own centre, shaping
the plastic mass as it will — that is Ovid, and that in a
way is Shakespeare. Perhaps this explains why we find
more of Ovid in Shakespeare than of any other ancient
poet.

VIII

GREEK CONCEPTIONS OF IMMORTALITY FROM HOMER TO PLATO

By HERBERT WEIR SMYTH

GREEK CONCEPTIONS OF IMMORTALITY FROM HOMER TO PLATO

To the primitive thought of most peoples the continued existence of the soul after death is an imperative
consequence of the recognition of the presence of the
soul in the living man. Uncivilized man cannot well
conceive the annihilation of the spirit that dwells within
him; and even the savage that has not attained to the
conception of "soul" refuses to believe that what is shall
utterly cease to be. The Greek race has left only a faint
record of the early stages of its culture. Its earliest literature testifies to a great civilization long over-past, and
assumes as self-evident the future life of the soul. It is my
purpose to trace the Greek conception of immortality
as it advances from the cruder faith of Homer to Plato's
triumphant proclamation of the divine nature of the
soul and its eternal union with God. Superstition in
its nobler and coarser forms, poetry, theology, mysticism,
and philosophy mould that conception in different degrees. The lower psychology recognizes mere continued
existence of the soul; the higher psychology attains to
the idea of personal immortality; grosser conceptions
refuse to surrender to higher forms of faith; more
highly developed notions coexist in the same age and
even in the same individual with notions derived from

an animistic stage of the evolution of religion; and while Greek thought in general accepts unquestioningly a life beyond the grave, agnosticism is not unknown in the later and complexer stages of thought and culture.

The Greek whose activity and thought are set forth in the Homeric poems regards the world as beautiful and just, controlled by higher powers, whose regulative action on life he accepts as inevitable, and whose favor alone enables him to secure the removal of his sense of human helplessness. But his modest demands are easily satisfied and he is too much engaged in action, he lives too much in the risks of adventure and the satisfaction of achievement, to give even unanalytic expression to a conscious joy in living; he is too unreflective even to mark the disproportionate share of good things that fall to the great, for whom alone the world, as his poetry, seems to exist. The epic poet too in his own degree has the constitutional aversion of his race to a "worship of sorrow," as Goethe called it; he keeps himself on the high and bright levels of the heroic world and its idealized figures, and rarely directs his glance to those sombre regions of actuality, where, with all its zest, life is beset by penury, weariness, and despair.

If pessimism is alien to Homer, he is still not altogether untroubled; but his gloomy utterances on the wretchedness of man's estate are scarcely the expression of disengaged reflection. Rather they are evoked by the situation he has in mind, as when he says "there is nothing more pitiful than man among all things that breathe and creep upon the earth"; or again, "few are the children like unto their sire, most are worse, and few are better." The early Hellene gains his buoyancy of spirit, his serenity, nay even (despite Plato) his very impulse to heroic endeavor, not only from his realization of the inevitableness of sorrow and of the cruelty of death, which awakens in him no thought of relief from suffering, but also, and perhaps in no small measure, from his cheerless view of the destination of his soul when once it has left its fleshly tenement.

To the ancient Greeks, as to other early peoples, the beginning of human life awakens no surprise. But death is of insistent interest. With the problem of life and death Homer deals as a poet, not as a psychologist. To his thinking man is dualistic or rather he exists in a double form; but Homer does not answer unequivocally the question: which is man's real self — his body, or his *psyche*, the "breath" in him, that quits the dying man from out of the barrier of his teeth, or through the stricken wound, and flits to Hades like a wreath of vapor. Primitive psychology may have deduced its belief in the conservation of the soul from the analogy of deathlike conditions which deprive man temporarily of consciousness. When sleep, the twin-brother of death, or swoon, or trance, has passed, an incorporeal element seems to return to the body which again becomes sentient. So in the permanent state of death, if the visible man perishes his soul is not destroyed because it does not return. The word for the "shade" of the dead (*eidolon*) is used also of the form that appears in dreams and of the wraith of the living man; but of any belief in the "dream-soul" that quits the body during sleep (a form of the astral body of the theosophists) Homer is ignorant. The analogy of the dream-state is to many primitive beliefs sufficient proof of the after-life of the soul; at any rate to the early Greek the content of dreams was not a mere illusive image, but a vivid, objective reality. The apparition in sleep of the dead to the living is warrant of their continued existence. Achilles *knows* that Patroclus has not been utterly destroyed: "all night long the soul of hapless Patroclus stood over me, wailing and lamenting, and wondrous like it was unto himself." For the dead are the disembodied counterparts of the living:

> Eternal form shall still divide
> The eternal soul from all beside;
> And I shall know him when we meet.

But there is no direct evidence that in the popular belief of the Homeric age the soul, which after death wears the form and feature of the living man, was thought to dwell within the body as his second-self, his *alter ego*, manifesting itself, when the activity of the body is suspended, only in dreams that foretell the future, and unnoticed in the waking hours when its functions are resumed. This is a conception that does not appear in definite form in Greece until the sixth century B.C. and as a tenet of Orphic faith.

When once the soul has passed the confines of the body, the eschatology of the Homeric age formulated for it a destiny that exceeds in gloom all visions of the other world ever evoked by the imagination of man, a future shaped into a profound and purposed contrast to a conception which equated life with the power to behold the radiant light of the sun. "Wherefore," says the shade of Teiresias to Odysseus in Hades, "wherefore hast thou left the light of the sun and come to behold the dead and a land alien to joy?" As Gruppe has said: "behind the misery in which he deems himself to live, the Homeric Greek beholds a greater, never-ending woe to come," a woe for all mankind without distinction of moral worth. For the good and the evil inhabit after death the same dread region. The implacable equity of retributive justice in another world is the product of later speculation, which has forced its way into Homer only in such passages as the prayer of Agamemnon:

Father Zeus, thou who rulest from Ida, most glorious and great, and thou Sun, who seest all things and hearest all things, and rivers and earth, and ye who beneath the earth punish the dead who have sworn falsely, be ye my witnesses.

The triad of great sinners, Tityus, Tantalus and Sisyphus, whose conscious torments in Hades are beheld by Odysseus, is not introduced as typical of the punishment of ordinary transgressors. Their offences, as their punishment, are exceptional. Homer knows of no hell, for Tartarus has not yet become the abode of suffering. Nor did the Greeks, as many other peoples, conceive of a hell until they had imagined a heaven.

If Homer had the constitutional tendency of his race to feel himself at home in this world, his view of the hereafter proves (as Napoleon said) that it is especially in the sphere of the imagination that the power of the unknown is immeasurable. Homeric imagination passes the uttermost margins of man's world and explores the awful demesnes of eternal dusk. Homer's view of the estate of the dead is not consistent; nor is that of his great successor whose apocalyptic vision beheld the regions of the *doloroso regno*.

Wearing the semblance of its bodily appearance either in normal life or as it was last seen upon the earth — the slain heroes clad in their gory armor — the soul passes across the river (either Oceanus or Styx) and enters Erebus, its destined abode, from which there is no return; though the poet does not expressly say that it abides there forever. A phantom prisoner in the dolorous mansions of the implacable Hades, in "a land of darkness, and where the light is of darkness," the soul lacks flesh, bones, and sinews; the power of motion it has, but it is motion devoid of purpose; it has voice, but only that of a squeak and gibber; it is of a filmy, vaporous nature, of no greater substantiality than a dream or an image mirrored in a glass, Some souls there are that possess intelligence and are affected by emotion; but most souls, unlike those of the great chieftains, have lost consciousness, memory, and will; they are devoid of intelligence because they do not know they are impalpable; they do not know what takes place in the upper world nor do they normally have any thought of the living; they are powerless to affect the living for good or for evil, as the living in turn cannot influence them for weal or woe; they cannot, as ghostly visitants, haunt the world above, and so helpless are they to avenge themselves, if murder has brought them to their loathed dwelling-place, that their kinsmen accept blood-money because they have no terror of their vengeful apparition.

In the gloom of Hades the shades live on in an unsubstantial reflection of their life in the "white world," a Russian phrase with a Greek ring to it. The phantom Orion still pursues his quarry, the phantom Minos still pronounces judgment; Achilles still is lord of all the dead, though he would fain exchange his shadowy dominion to be a bondsman of the glebe in the world of reality. Kingship does not die, and eternal serfdom awaits the slave.

It is rather continued existence than immortal life that the Homeric man expects will be the portion of his soul. To this belief the exceptions are only the expressions of the Homeric fancy resting upon some "halb verklungne Sage," which seeks to discover an exemption from the common doom of mankind. Homer has preserved a trace of the belief that certain privileged classes have superior expectations as to future happiness, a belief that still exists among some undeveloped peoples, as the Peruvians and the inhabitants of the Tonga Islands, and which, in a higher state of society, prompted the remark of the lady of quality that "they will think twice before they refuse a person of my condition." But in Homer's unconscious reminiscence of hero-worship, it is not signal merit, or exceeding virtue, or even superior earthly station, but the autocratic will of the gods, that unexpectedly frees a chosen few (and these only men of the far-off past) from the necessity of passing through the gates of death; and thus ensures them a perpetuation of that complete existence, which, in the belief of his age, lay in the undissevered coexistence of soul and body. It is surpassing beauty, as in the case of Ganymede or Tithonus, or privileged estate as the husband of a mortal woman beloved by a god or sprung from a god, as in the case of Menelaos, the son-in-law of Zeus, that justifies translation to Olympus, to exclusive divine companionship in the miraculous island of Aea, or to the Elysian Fields at the end of the earth by the shore of Ocean, where the recipients of the miraculous favor of the gods pass their days in eternal joy. In the Islands of the Blest, Hesiod's designation of the Elysian Fields, the same felicity awaits the race of heroes, the demigods; and so in Assyrian and Babylonian myths a few heroes escape death by removal to islands of the blessed. In the primitive Greek conception this immortality is alone the gift of the gods: to live forever with soul and body undivorced is to become a *god;* though the divinity clothing the elect is in so far incomplete that it does not confer the power to revisit the land of the living. Nor do the translated enjoy any cult on the part of the living because they are powerless to affect men on earth either for good or for evil.

Translation to Elysium or the Blessed Isles, the fabric of the poet's imagination, did indeed in a later period of Greek life continue to appeal to the popular fancy:

> Harmodius, our darling, thou art not dead!
> Thou liv'st in the isles of the blest, 't is said,
>   With Achilles first in speed
>   And Tydides Diomede.
>
> CONINGTON.

But this poetic fiction had no appreciable result in modifying the actual faith of the ordinary man in the classical period; nor indeed in a much later age did it do more than supply the imagery of the hereafter.

> Thou art not dead, my Protè! Thou art flown
> To a far country better than our own;
> Thy home is now an Island of the Blest;
> There 'mid Elysian meadows take thy rest.
>
> SYMONDS.

It awakened no general hope and in Homer is simply a gleam of light cast upon the dark background of man's destiny.

What reason is there that the Greeks of the Homeric age should have a conception of the other life colored to so profound a sadness? It cannot be that it is a transference to Hades of any sadness with which they viewed their life upon the earth and deepened by the shadows of approaching doom. The sorrow of this world is indeed due to the direct agency of the aristocratic gods who live at ease and are careless of mankind, who have two urns of evil and only one of good, whose arbitrary will is the cause of actions and motives in men that otherwise remain inexplicable. The sorrow of this world is only an undercurrent of belief never depressing the joy of life to a lower level than serene gravity.

It is the absence of all cult of the spirits of the dead that conditions the Homeric eschatology. Homer's conception of the dead represents a rationalistic interruption of ancestor-worship, a cult existing in the age anterior to the epic, and reappearing in Greece proper when the period of the epic had passed.

In the Mycenaean age, which lasted till about the twelfth century, soul-cult is attested by the entombed arms and utensils, by the traces of sacrifice of animals and of human beings, by the round altar open at the bottom for the passage of sacrificial blood, which the graves excavated by Schliemann at Mycenae itself have disclosed, and by similar discoveries at the Dipylon in Athens and in Crete. It is a reasonable inference that the Greeks of the Mycenaean period had the consolation that personality would at least be continued in the family or clan, that the regular observance of sacrifices to the dead was a symbol of the uninterrupted life of the soul. To the people which has left such testimony to the cult of their dead these dead must have been not mere shades but sentient ghosts, taking delight in offerings made at their tombs near which they lingered, rejoicing in funeral games in their honor, ghosts who dispensed good to the living, who defended their kin from evil; but who, if the sacrifices in their honor were omitted, would be compelled to leave their graves as vampires (for the sacrifice of blood points to vampirism) and become endowed with the dread power of haunting their enemies; nevertheless capable of conciliation and appeasement by pious ministrations.

And yet Homer has not altogether lost trace of this cult of souls; though such recollections as are embedded in *Iliad* and *Odyssey* are no indication of contemporary acceptance of the religious beliefs of which they were originally the expression. A funeral feast is held in honor of Patroclus before the cremation of his body, human beings and animals are sacrificed upon his pyre, jars of honey and oil, recalling the embalming (and inhumation) of the dead, are placed beside the pyre, and funeral games follow the burning of the corpse; again, the arms of Eëtion and Elpenor are burned; Odysseus pours libations to the dead and makes sacrifices of the blood of victims to reanimate for a brief space of time the faint spirits of the querulous shades in Hades.

To these indications of the submergence of soul-cult in the age of Homer, others may be added of still slighter cogency. But the fact remains — the proper belief of that age rejects the worship of dead souls. The tendance of the spirits of the departed that marked the Mycenaean age has given place to utter neglect.

In the causes of this interruption of the earlier belief the student of Greek religion and of ethnology is alike interested. The interruption will not have been sudden according to all well-understood analogies; and there is ample time for the subsidence of one faith and the rise of another between the fall of the Mycenaean civilization and the civilization limned in Homer, who pictures the earlier society as already verging towards its decline. Can the neglect of the cult of the dead in Homer be the result of the substitution of incineration for inhumation?

In Homer all the dead, heroes and commonalty alike, are burned. No shade may reach its abode in Hades until its body has been consumed by fire. When the shade of Patroclus appears to Achilles asleep during the night after Hector has been slain, it says to him:

So thou dost sleep, Achilles, but me thou hast forgotten. Not when I lived wast thou unmindful of me, but now that I am dead. Make haste and bury me that I pass the gates of Hades. The spirits keep me far aloof, the phantoms of the

weary dead, nor suffer me yet to mingle with them beyond the
River; and vainly do I roam around the wide-gated house of
Hades. Nay give me thy hand, I pitifully entreat thee, for
never more again shall I return from Hades when ye have
given me my due of fire.

As with Patroclus so with Elpenor — so long as the
body of the dead was unburnt it still was sentient.
Cicero says that to his thinking Hector's body before it
was consumed by fire could still feel the outrage done
to it by Achilles.

Of the welfare of the souls of the dead the Homeric
age seems to have no other thought except to secure to
them absolute separation from earth and eternal sojourn
in Hades, and even this thought of them seems to be
dictated by the desire to remove from the survivors the
malign suggestion that *their* spirits will, if endowed with
partial consciousness through failure to destroy the body
by fire, be forced to undergo a fate more awful than
Hades itself — to hover eternally in unrest between
the world of the living and the world of the dead.

There are no ghosts in Homer — *de non apparentibus
et non existentibus eadem est ratio.* The total destruction
of the body by fire and the absence of remains near
which the spirit of the dead might linger removes from
the living the dread that their dreams may be haunted
by apparitions of departed friends and foes (the
Homeric man dreams only of those he knows.) If the
address of the shade of Patroclus to Achilles is inter-

preted to imply the capacity of the dead soul to injure the living it must be regarded as a survival of the earlier belief though it is found in one of the latest books of the *Iliad* — not as the opinion of the Homeric age; and Elpenor's warning to Odysseus not to leave his body unburned does not imply that that age feared the visitation of a neglected spirit.

The coexistence in Homer of the custom of cremating the dead with the disappearance of the older belief in the puissance of departed souls has been explained by many scholars as due to the substitution of cremation for inhumation because of the dread of the Greeks, in the period of the pre-historic migrations in the last quarter of the second millennium before Christ, that their kin if interred in their homes in the Greek mainland which they were abandoning for a new dwelling place across the Aegean, might become the prey of enemies, dogs, and birds. But this suggestion is no more tenable than the other that the migrating peoples feared lest the remains of their dead kin should be used for magical charms against the surviving members of the clan. Or did the new rite arise in Asia Minor among the colonists, the ancestors of the Homeric Greeks, who feared that enemies would desecrate the graves of their dead while they were winning a foothold in an alien country and had no fixed abode? Or were the dead regarded as vampires to be put to rest by burning — a belief that has scant support from Homer? Dr. Dörpfeld would have

us believe (on slight evidence) that the processes of inhumation and incineration were closely connected, that
while the dead in early times were always buried, their
bodies were embalmed or scorched, and that the latter
process might be carried so far as complete burning, especially in the cases of those who died on foreign soil
and wished to be interred at home.

Many theories, little certainty. The connection of
the practice of cremation with the ultimate destination
of the soul is a problem that must be surrendered by
the Hellenist to the anthropologist. It is ill-advised to
isolate the substitution of cremation for interment among
the Greeks of the Homeric age from the like phenomenon among the Celts and the worshippers of Odin, who
shared the belief of the Homeric Greeks that with the
burning of the body the soul departs to another world.
Professor Ridgeway indeed claims that the appearance
of the doctrine of the soul's passage to a spirit-world
is coincident with the intrusion into Greece of the
Achaeans, a northern people, who brought with them
the practice of cremation and the belief that there
was a separate habitation for departed spirits, and
that this practice and belief was superimposed upon
that of the indigenous population of Greece which
thought that the spirit lingered in or near the place
where its carnal tenement was buried in the earth.

Whatever their ultimate connection, the two facts
of the burning of the dead and the atrophy of the cult

of their souls are established for the civilization depicted in Homer. From the eleventh to the ninth or eighth century, so far as we can discover from his epics, men were concerned with the question of the future life of the soul from the point of view of the living; and in the absence of any service to the dead the result was inevitable that their spirits should be regarded as ineffective, and that the thought men take of the departed should gradually fade away with personal memory. There was "no resurrection in the minds of men." Only the phantom solace remained for the great that their deeds should live immortal through the poet's art. For the common man there was no solace whatever.

But the horizon of Greek faith was not everywhere nor for all time bounded by the doctrine of Homer. The older worship of souls still survived in Greece proper. It is attested in Hesiod. It is attested by the beehive tomb at Menidi in Attica in which six skeletons were discovered surrounded by funeral offerings, while in the approach to the sepulchre fragments of pottery, showing an uninterrupted series of Mycenaean, Dipylon, and black and red figured Attic vases, prove that the tomb had been visited by successive generations to whom we must attribute the belief that the spirits of the dead were still conscious and potent, not forever removed from participation in the life of their kindred. This belief may well have continued throughout the Homeric age in undetected localities, even of the Asiatic littoral, among classes of society untouched by the creed of the epic minstrels. It is certain that when we enter upon the historic age we have evidence of the repristination, if not the continuance, of the pre-Homeric eschatology.

For the earliest part of the historic age our evidence indeed is scant. But for the classical period, thanks to the testimony of the late lyric, Attic literature, and sepulchral monuments, we can form a tolerably definite conception of the actual belief of the Greeks of the fifth and fourth centuries. Eliminating such superstitious beliefs as that recorded by Plato to the effect that if there was a gale of wind when a man was dying it might blow his soul away altogether, let us endeavor to discover what the average Athenian thought would become of his disembodied spirit, if he was neither a member of a mystical sect nor tinged with philosophy.

In the first place it made no difference to that spirit whether its body was interred or burned. Both methods were in vogue, but inhumation was the commoner. The soul survived, possessing consciousness; it could use the various utensils and other objects deposited by the remains; it had the appetites and the grosser passions of the body; it partook of the funeral baked meats prepared by the family on its return from the grave ; and it had a special meal for itself served at the tomb on the third and ninth day after the burial. On the thirtieth of the month there was a "service," and each year the birthday of the deceased was celebrated with sacrifices. Offerings and observances alike aimed to secure contentment in death for the souls in their abode in the tomb, from which in springtime (and ordinarily only at the "festival of flowers") they were all thought to ascend into the habitation of their living kin, who accordingly decreed in their honor the festival of "all souls," thus anticipating the celebration of that name instituted by the Abbot of Cluny in the tenth century. The spirit-visitors swarmed into the houses of their kin, there they were entertained, and thence they were finally driven out with a cry much like that in vogue in Rome — *manes exite paterni* —, or in Slavonic lands — "ye have eaten and drunken, souls, now go, now go."

The offices of the cult of the dead, as the spirit itself, were intimately attached to the tomb where the remains reposed. The dead became earth-spirits (*chthonioi*), and dwelt in the demesne of the earth-gods; they hovered round their tombs, alike whether they were good or evil spirits; they were conscious of what happened on earth and knew whether the passer-by was friend or foe; they might assume visible form, especially that of snakes. Usually however they remained invisible, though endowed with the sense of hearing and, when they were near, *de mortuis nil nisi bonum*, the original meaning of which saying derived its significance from the fact that any one who spoke evil of a deceased person was liable to prosecution by his descendants, who would otherwise be visited with the wrath of the dead. In very late times we hear of souls conjured up by necromancers (as the ghost of Samuel by the witch of Endor), who, so Plutarch tells, made use of phantoms to cheat the credulous. The ordinary method of converse with the spirit-world was by incubation, the dead appearing in dreams to the visitors at "soul-conjuring" places.

In common belief the dead became invisible powers called "the higher and the better," or more generally "the blessed," like the German "die Seligen." Popular eschatology did not dogmatize about their estate. It expressed itself in terms of the relation of the dead to their descendants, for the well-being of the soul was conditioned, not by its deeds in this life, but by the worship paid it by its kin. The solidarity of the family was in turn supported by the cult of the dead. What concerned their living kinsmen, actual or adopted, was, apart from natural piety, the attitude that the spirits would take toward themselves. Were they to bring fruitfulness to fields and to marriage, were they to be helpers in time of trouble, and especially when their kin or countrymen in whose territory their remains reposed were hard pressed in battle? In the *Libation-Bearers* of Aeschylus and the *Electra* of Sophocles the shade of the murdered Agamemnon is implored to aid his children in their purpose to requite his foul murder upon the faithless Clytaemnestra and her paramour Aegisthus; and at the same time the deprivation of accustomed sacrifices is held over him *in terrorem*. So in the first named play, from Campbell's version: —

> *Orestes.* My father, king in all but in thy death,
> I pray for power to rule thine ancient hall.
> *Electra.* I too, my father, with a daughter's voice,
> Pray thee for power to work Aegisthus woe.
> *Orestes.* So men shall honour thee with sacrifice
> And righteous banquets; else tne savoury smoke
> That streams on earth for souls more fortunate,
> Shall leave thee comfortless.

Or, on the other hand, were the souls of the dead to become workers of ill who would visit their enemies with terrifying dreams, who would become spirits of curse and, with "memory as their ally," bring epilepsy, apoplexy, sudden death and distress of every kind even upon the unborn descendants of those who had injured them in life or who had neglected to minister to their ghostly welfare? "Have you never remarked," says Xenophon in the *Cyropaedia*, "what terrors the souls of those who have suffered an unjust death strike into those who are stained with their blood, and what avenging deities they send upon impious offenders? Do you imagine, too, that the honors offered to the dead would still continue, if their souls possessed no power?"

If the Attic cult of the dead looks largely to the benefit to accrue to the living in accordance with the *do ut des* doctrine of undeveloped Greek ethics, we must not underestimate, as is too often done by students of Hellenic folk-lore, the large part played by the im-

pulses of natural affection. "The dust does not hide
the noble grace of their living kinsmen," says Pindar;
Orestes and Electra demand the punishment of Clytaemnestra and Aegisthus less for their own sakes than
for their murdered father's; Antigone's love for her
unburied brother to whom she gives the rites of sepulture
costs her her own life; and in the face of threats and in
the expectation of exile Teucer demands the burial of
Ajax.

The family alone preserved the cult of its dead. In
the family the souls of the departed were worshipped as
puissant ghosts and became in time akin to the spirits
of the heroes, a special class of men either actually ancestors, or fictitiously regarded as ancestors, of tribes
or clans. Primarily the heroes were the legendary
princes of the tales of Troy and Thebes, in later times
founders of cities, kings, famous athletes, and, by a
gradual extension of the term, men in general distinguished for great ability and for virtues, in which, however, morality was not necessarily included. In the
latest times any deceased person might be called a hero.
In the classical period, however, the heroes who had
been men of distinction were thought to enjoy after
death a higher form of existence and thus received special
reverence from the living because of their signal power
to avert calamity and to render help in time of danger
to the district sanctified by the possession of their tombs.
The cult of heroes is often not to be distinguished from

that of the common dead; but the bodies of the former were often buried in the market-place or under an altar to some god or by the hearth, but only the common dead (who might not be buried within the city) enjoyed the ministrations of the family, the primal social unit.

In later times the line of demarcation between hero and god was often obliterated in popular consciousness though language differentiated between their cult; of a god the proper words for altar and sacrifice were βωμός and θύειν; while ἐσχάρα and ἐναγίζειν were applied in the case of heroes. The souls not merely of the heroes but of the ordinary dead came in course of time to be regarded as gods. But the Greeks did not develop the idea of family gods. The nearest approach on Greek soil to the *lar familiaris* is the " good spirit, " the ἀγαθὸς δαίμων, originally the spirit of an ancestor and the object of reverence to the family.

The popular faith in the continued potency of the soul was perhaps stronger in the eighth and seventh centuries than in the later classical period which I have, in general, been describing. And yet though that faith was prevailingly held in most classes of society in the Periclean age and a century later in the age of Demosthenes, as is attested by the evidence of literature and the funereal vases; though it afforded the living at least the consolation of the belief that the spirits of their dear ones were not cast into the cavernous darkness of Hades but tarried in or near the place of their interment, that faith does not indicate any profound conviction of the happiness of the departed, nor, through its vagueness of outline, did it possess an authority potent enough to displace the old-time concrete associations engrafted upon religious belief by the power of the sovereign poet who controlled in large measure the imagination of posterity. As Homer conceived the greater gods, so they were incorporated into the public faith of Hellas; as Homer pictured the abode of souls in the realm of Hades, so successive generations in the most enlightened age gazed into a world beyond. In part, and especially in literature, men expressed their belief in terms of conscious recourse to Homer (for Homer colored even the form of thought), in part also Homer's eschatology still actually survived, though properly irreconcilable with the dominant conceptions which gave a higher evaluation to the dignity of life.

A reconciliation was however affected and with a disdain of logic that marks a religion resisting the oppression of a theology that systematically casts aside the more primitive lineaments of popular conception. Upon the current belief that the souls of all the dead, whether buried or burned, were free and hovered in or near their tombs, possessing potency for good or evil, was superimposed the Homeric doctrine of a separate and common abode for those whose bodies had been consumed by fire, impotent souls, confined to the house of Hades. The mourner at the tomb, accepting unconsciously a compromise, believed (it seems) that his appeal would gradually reach the dull cold ear of death, and that the soul of the departed in its subterranean abode in Hades would respond to his call, and, ascending to the grave, be near at hand to receive the ministrations of those it loved. The coalescence of the Homeric and the later belief enables us to understand the equation of the grave with Hades, as in Sophocles' expression "to lie in Hades." Whatever the faith of the unlettered, literature proves that the Homeric vision of the other world had not suffered supersession. The tragic poets and Plato retain to a large extent the places and persons of the Homeric Hades — Styx, Acheron, Pyriphlegethon, Cocytus, Minos and Rhadamanthys; but Tartarus is changed and is now a place of torture. At times too the dead is regarded sometimes as dwelling in Hades among the good (in accordance with Pindar's more cheerful view of the hereafter), or among the pious in Elysium, or even as transferred, like Harmodius and Aristogeiton, to the Islands of the Blest. Aeschylus' conception of the future life is largely Homeric; though his persistent religious and ethical purpose leads him to accentuate the un-Homeric idea of future punishment that had been developed in the sixth century, and to dwell on the torments of the guilty in the hands of the avenging Furies. Sophocles, the "most Homeric" of the tragic poets, often represents Homer's view of the dead; he rarely touches the doctrine of retribution, and (except where he reproduces Orphic conceptions) makes only a slight advance beyond Aeschylus in regard to future happiness. Euripides is familiar with the fear of punishment and the hope of reward; as in a fragment where he says "whoever honors his parents in life, both in life and in death is dear unto the gods." But the doctrine of retributive punishment expressed in terms of the Homeric Hades filled men with terror from which the current faith based on the cult of the dead, had it been absolute, might have delivered them, and from which they were delivered by Epicurus, according to his passionate Roman disciple. "When a man" says the aged Cephalus in the *Republic*, "when a man faces the thought that he is going to die, he becomes afraid and concerned about things for which he did not care before. For the stories (which he laughed at before) about those in Hades, that the man who has done wrong here must pay the penalty for it in the other world, these stories torment his soul lest they may prove to be true."

In the brilliant period of Athens' history men hoped, and feared, vacillated, and doubted. Riper culture was affecting a cleavage of classes. The more enlightened may have got some notion of theological and philosophical speculation, but until Plato developed his doctrines the adherents of the traditionary theology did not conceive the soul to be eternal and indestructible. As for the masses, Aristotle expressly says they were uncertain whether the soul perished or was immortal. What answer then could the Hellene make to the obstinate questioning

> Cease they to love, and move, and breathe, and speak,
> Who die?

Tragedy is strangely silent, strangely inconsistent. Aeschylus offers little, and Sophocles only slightly more, evidence of the belief that the dead had feeling and consciousness. In one of his plays the former poet makes one of his characters utter the sentiment "if thou wishest to do good or ill to the dead, it is indifferent because they have neither joy nor pain." And yet, in the *Agamemnon*, the demon of the race of Tantalus, the fanatical murderess of the king, declares with savage frenzy that her child whom he had slain, "Iphigenia, his daughter, as is her right, will gladly meet her father by the swift-flowing stream of woes and throw her arms about him and kiss him." Nor is the expectation of a reunion in the world below foreign to Sophocles, whose self-blinded Oedipus declares "had I sight, I know not with what eyes I could ever have gazed upon my father, when I had come to Hades, or upon my wretched mother, since I have sinned against both such sins as deserve punishment more severe than strangling." Antigone's love for her brother is not to be limited to the world where she dares and suffers for him. She will love him, for love she must, even among the dead, where she will also share the home of her unfortunate parents: "But

I feed myself with good hope that my coming will be welcome to my father, and pleasant to thee, my mother, and welcome to thee, my darling brother."

To the searching mind of Euripides, the poet of Greece's great Age of Doubt, thought in all its aspects made effective appeal. At all cost to artistic propriety he would give voice to the jangling of beliefs: he had his heroic personages at hand, imposed upon him by his conventional art; their august mouths should bear the message of his self-contentions and the hesitations of the time's decaying faith. He hallows the sanctities of the faith of his fathers in the *Alcestis*, fairly a romantic play, but rooted in popular doctrine: here Death himself battles for the life of that "blessed spirit" of measureless self-surrender; Megara calls upon the soul of her husband to hear her from the tomb and to come to her aid. But it is not a real faith that he enstages: it is the faith of a literary opportunist, conscious of the pressure of tradition and of the convenience of recourse to accredited forms of expression, but in still greater degree conscious of the exigencies of dramatic interest. But behind even this conventionalized orthodoxy there lurks the rationalist. "We prove ourselves," says the poet of the *Hippolytus*, "in truth mad lovers of this, whate'er this be, that glitters on the earth, because we know no other life and things beneath the earth are not revealed. We are borne along at random by illusions." And in darker mood: "The dead are earth and shadow, void of feeling"; "not to be born and to be dead are one." If the mobile affinities of Euripides rested for a moment upon the doctrines of the Orphics and the Pythagoreans, they found a larger sympathy with a belief, unassailed by the poet, as are his other beliefs, that proves him not to have been utterly unstable in his conception of the destiny of the soul. Popular fancy, theology, philosophy, and poetry have all contributed something to the idea that the spirit ascends to the aether, the "heaven" of an age to whom the gods had long since ceased to dwell on Olympus. "Earth to earth, the spirit to the region above," Epicharmus had said, not without some reference to the popular identification of the soul with the air or aether. It is difficult to determine how far such ideas were influenced by the dualistic conception that the universe consisted of "earth" and of "aether" as the active intelligent element. With Diogenes of Apollonia's equation of aether with soul Euripides is familiar, and in the *Helen* says that "albeit the mind of the dead does not live, it still has deathless consciousness when merged in deathless aether." Pantheistic absorption into the All leaves no place for the persistence of individuality, the essence of true immortality.

The orators do not scruple to doubt whether the spirits of the dead possess consciousness; in all the orations delivered on state occasions in honor of those who gave their lives for their country there is heard no note of the recognition of kindred in the other life.

Even Socrates, a confirmed optimist, had no fixed belief whether he will become as naught and have no consciousness of anything, or whether there is a removal of the soul from this place to some other, where, they say, the great men of old enjoy immortality — both are alike good, the one will be like a dreamless sleep, the other will afford him the happiness of conversing with Homer and Agamemnon and Odysseus. Where all are ignorant how can he know? Socrates' vision of the future life is more akin to Homer's than it is to that of the theological poets of Greece; and it is in the main that of the average man of intelligence of his day.

It is naturally alien to that of the philosophers with whose physical researches Socrates had scant sympathy. From the Ionic philosophy men could derive no confirmation of a hope in the continued existence or the immortality of the individual soul. To that philosophy the soul is merely a part of nature, a form of the universal force animating the primal substance out of which the world was formed and energizing in all things. On such a view the soul is indeed divine by reason of the fact that it is a portion of that cosmic force which formed and guides the universe; but it does not exist for itself and has no individual existence. As has been well said, the Ionian philosophy almost lost sight of man in its endeavor to fathom the nature of the universe and the phenomena of life. Heraclitus admits only the immortality of the principle pervading the universe; to him the soul is fire, the type of all-pervasive motion; for the statements ascribing to him the belief that the individual soul continued to exist after death are derived from Platonizing thinkers. His proper teaching denies the absolute death of the soul, for death is birth as birth is death. If in general the Eleatics, maintaining Being to be an indissoluble One, regard the soul as a condition of activity of associated elements, Parmenides shows traces of the belief that the soul had perished before it entered the body and lives on after its dissolution. But herein he, and to a still greater degree Empedocles and Pythagoras, show the influence of Orphism. Democritus lets the atoms, which unite to form the soul, disappear with the death of the body into the constituent parts of the universe. The dualist Anaxagoras regards *nous*, which "arranges all things," as incorporeal, possessed of the power of will and thought, all-wise, transcendent, though it may inhere in certain things as men, animals, and plants. But individuality is only a form of the universal. Separation of the body is the death of the soul. At death only the *nous* survives, while the soul disappears since it is only a manifestation of the *nous*. Personality is only a form of something more general which vitalizes the body; a single form, possessing no independence of itself, cannot continue forever.

But any philosophy which regarded as impersonal the only true reality and left no room for human personality cannot well be the cause of the general silence, before Plato, as to any hope of true immortality. The figuration of souls on works of art in the form of doves, bees, serpents, or as tiny creatures often with human heads, testifies merely to the popular belief in their continued existence, not to any true immortality; a belief which, at different times, had created out of dead souls the mythological conceptions of the Keres, Moerae, Harpies, and Sirens. Even the reliefs supposed to depict the feast of the dead in Elysium are more safely interpreted as referring to the funeral banquet of the living. In the funereal stelae and lecythi, expressions of love of kin, of piety and tenderness toward the dead, the clasped hands, the incomparable salutation and farewell ($\chi a\hat{i}\rho\epsilon$) that binds life and death so closely together, do not have regard to a world beyond the life in which love with all its griefs clings to love only through remembrance:

I am not lost when Love remembers me.

This silence is all the more strange because that age was not unfamiliar with the hope of a higher, a personal immortality. It may be that love needed no deeper expression than the monument intended to serve as a lasting memorial of piety and to symbolize life continued after death; it may be that men were reticent because of a certain delicacy of reserve and held themselves so aloof from the profession of their hope that it could not be reflected in literature or art. Certain it is, however, that in at least one of the two Mysteries a fixed hope of personal immortality was born.

Both the Eleusinian and the Orphic Mysteries reflect in terms of a quickened religious impulse and a profounder and less external faith, that upheaval in the old order of things in society, in politics, in justice, in the manifold relations of life, which marks the period of transition from the Homeric age to the middle of the seventh century B.C. The ends and aims of life had grown more complex; love and hate were not such simple passions, the naïve beliefs in things divine and human were changing their old-time aspects. Forms of belief that had remained quiescent were now seen to be changed with a fructifying power to minister to the claims of an individualism that sought satisfaction for its deeper needs and visible evidence, in religious rites, of the realization of those needs. Ecstacy of religious fervor, exaltation of soul, brought men into nearer communion with the divine, and with it a large consolation that rescued them alike from the traditional belief imposed by the authority of Homer and from the unsubstantial conceptions of their future estate inherent in the popular worship of souls; perhaps also from the newer doctrines of philosophy that left no room for personal solace. It was in and through the Mysteries that men sought to find an anodyne for the misery of this world and a greater hope as regards the world to come. Sectaries alone could assault the public religion of Hellas at its

strongest point — the perfect freedom of its faith and
its universal appeal to every Hellene. Both the Eleusinian and the Orphic Mysteries are sectarian — they
promised salvation to their devotees alone; they granted
no hope to the unregenerate.

From the narrow circle of believers at Eleusis the
faith spread to all who accepted the mysterious teaching inculcated in connection with the worship of Demeter, Korè, and Triptolemus, divinities of the earth
alike the source of life and the place of the dead. Purification, according to ritual, of all who could speak
Greek and who had not shed human blood, was the only
preliminary requisite for initiation into the mysteries of
Eleusis. These, we know, comprised dramatic spectacles,
which probably envisaged the seizure of Persephone,
the distress of her mother, and the passion of Dionysus
— Iacchus; secondly, the display of sacred objects; and,
thirdly, the utterance of certain words by the hierophant. Whatever may have been the nature of these
aspects of the ritual, whatever the character of the symbolism (the planting of the seed and the birth of vegetation is surely *not* an analogy to the death of the body
and the continued existence of the soul), the essential
feature of the cult is not a mystery: it was the reverential
and unquestioning acceptance of the word of the goddess of Earth, who, when her daughter was saved to her
for two parts of the year from her dread lord, had first revealed the "manner of her rites" and taught her "holy

mysteries" to Eleusis' king. "Happy," said she, "is he among mortal men who hath gazed upon these things. And he that is uninitiate and hath no lot in them, hath never equal lot in death beneath the murky gloom."

Though the Eleusinian Mysteries may have ministered solace to the individual (death is a blessing, not an evil, is the utterance of a hierophant), they did not possess the vital force for spiritual regeneration that marks the Mysteries of the narrower sect of the devotees of Orpheus. It was the function of the Mysteries of Eleusis not to prove a future life, but to define the state of existence after death; and even that lacks precision of outline. A system of positive doctrine was not set forth at Eleusis. The initiates, Aristotle expressly tells us, did not have to learn anything; they were to be "affected and put into a frame of mind." It is therefore doubtful whether they received the assurance of personal immortality.

It was the Orphic Mysteries that gave birth to the most profound ideas in Greek religion, — the divine origin of the soul, its eternal nature, and personal immortality, — doctrines reproduced by Pindar along with the traditionary theology; professed with passion by Empedocles, at once poet, physicist, and mystic; established as the rule of life by the Pythagorean order, but not touching the general profession of belief; and finally intellectualized when they were taken over by Plato, who fused metaphysics with theology. With

Plato the great spiritualistic movement of Hellas reached its culmination.

Great movements in religion are paradoxes to current belief or conduct. Orphism regarded the world, not as beautiful and regulated by the justice of the old-time gods, but as evil because of the implication in man of impulses that are the spring of unhappiness. The rise of Orphism came at a moment of religious readjustment when men were not merely returning to an unrealized or half-realized doctrine, as in a modern "revival"; men had come to the realization that the moral order of the world did not fulfill itself completely in this life; they were endeavoring to find, through emotional expansion rather than through a sustained effort of the reasoning intelligence, a new faith that should satisfy the craving of the soul by pointing to redemption from sin, and how, through its own conscious effort in purification, the soul might reunite with God. The continuation of the life of the individual after death had become an imperative ethical postulate.

Of the influences that worked to awaken this faith the most potent was the worship of Dionysus, a newcomer in the Olympian hierarchy. Other localities besides Thrace adopted his cult, but it was from Thrace especially that, as early as the seventh century, there was diffused throughout Greece the worship of the god of spiritual regeneration. In the enthusiastic exaltation of the cult of the god of dying and reviving vegetation lay the germ of the Greek belief in true immortality. It is to Dionysus that the poet Melanippides cries: "Hear me, oh father, wonder of mortal men, thou that carest for my ever-living soul"; and it is in the spirit of the Orphic faith that Euripides asks

> Who knows but death may be what men call life,
> And life be dying?

The devotees of the mythical Thracian priest Orpheus stood outside the formal religion of the State, which never admitted a system of strict dogmatic doctrine. Their teaching united theology and ethics in its conception that faith in immortality was a motive force for moral regeneration. The soul before it came to reside in man was godlike and endowed with heavenly purity; and of its divine nature it was forever conscious. To the guards that stand before the pool of Memory in the lower world, the soul must say, when it comes thither, in the words prescribed by the Book of the Dead: "I am the child of earth and the starry heaven; but I (that is, my soul) am of celestial descent." So too when it appears before Persephone, the supreme judge, it says: "Pure and born of the pure I come before you, Queen of those who dwell in the lower world, Eucles, Eubuleus, and ye other immortal gods — for I claim that I, too, am of your immortal race."

It would be of interest to deal at close range with the physiological element in the Orphic doctrine that the soul is divine. But I must leave to others the determination of the question whether the phenomenon of mystic exaltation or the phenomenon of sleep contributed to the formation of that belief. On the one hand there are the tumultuous dance, the frenzied shouts, the rending of the victim, the devouring of its raw flesh, the drinking of its blood, — all the spiritual intoxication (ἔκστασις, μανία) of the "sleepless bacchants" of the rites of Dionysus. In moments of such ecstatic excitement it may be held that the "possessed" soul departs from the body, and that its return indicates that a temporary union with the god of the mystic rite has taken place; but there is also reason for the thought that in such abnormal states it is in reality the body that has been "possessed" and that the god is in the bacchant. Perhaps in the lethargy of exhaustion ensuing upon frenzy the apparent absence of the soul might suggest the idea of its sojourn with the gods.

Be this as it may, we have actual testimony to the notion that while we are awake the soul is asleep, and that when we are sunk in sleep (the counterfeit presentment of death) the soul is awake and manifests a power of which it is incapable when the body is active. This belief is explicitly set forth by Pindar, one of our early authorities for Orphism:

The body of all men is subject to all-powerful death, but there still remains alive the image (εἴδωλον) of life; for that alone is from the gods. It sleeps while the limbs are active, but to those in sleep it reveals in many dreams a coming award of joy and sorrow.

This idea appears in Aeschylus, Plato, and Aristotle; but here is the first occurrence of the argument that the soul survives the death of the body because it is of divine origin.

But to return to the doctrines of the Orphics, which were modified in part by the teachings of Pythagoras. When the soul, which as a god had dwelt with the gods, reaches the earth having passed the gates of the seven planetary spheres, it is immured in the body, its grave or prison-house. An "exile and wanderer from God," it is now bound in the fatal "circle" or "wheel of generation," and must undergo a series of births and deaths, assuming the form even of animals, fish, or plants if it has not purified itself sufficiently in a former life to warrant a higher state. Metempsychosis is thus indissolubly associated with purification. At each death the soul passes into Hades, where it enters upon an intermediate condition of reward or punishment. It was in the exclusive circle of the Orphic sectaries that there came into existence, for the first time in the history of European thought, the doctrine of future retributive justice. If the soul has purified itself to a certain degree, Elysium is its appointed residence, and there, in the sunlight of that nether paradise, in the "beautiful meadow around fairflowing Acheron," it enjoys an existence representing all the delights of its terrene state. The joys of this heaven are depicted by Pindar in a fashion that recalls certain modern hymns:

For them shineth below the strength of the sun while in
our world it is night, and the space of crimson-flowered
meadows before their city is full of the shade of frankincense-
trees, and of fruits of gold. And some in horses, and in bodily
feats, and some in dice, and some in harp-playing have delight; and among them thriveth fair-flowering bliss; and
fragrance streameth ever through the lovely land, as they
mingle incense of every kind upon the altars of the gods.—
MYERS' translation, frag. 129.

After ten rebirths and ten periods of sojourn below,
if the soul has expiated its "ancient guilt" by living
in purity, it is finally freed from the prison-house of
the body, and returns to its celestial home. If it proves
itself incapable of expiation and atonement it is cast
into Tartarus. With a heaven has come a hell.

The cardinal doctrine of Orphism is, in a word, that
man cannot save himself except by submission; only
through purification and "fasting from evil" can the
soul regain its original purity and divine nature. The
soul preserves in the hereafter its personality unimpaired, a doctrine upon which some modern philosophers have laid much stress as a necessary sequel to
the affirmation of individuality in this life.

Plato is at once theologian and metaphysician. With
his own theory of Ideas he has (imperfectly in part) cor-
related the doctrine of the future state of the soul that
he received from Orphism and Pythagoreanism. To him
philosophy has become a sort of initiation into the
mysteries, a release and purification from the senses.

The soul, or more strictly its sovereign rational part, comes from God. It is independent of the body, the source of its power of motion, it is spiritual, individual, and immortal. Reason is the "eye of the soul," and is "akin to the divine, and immortal, and ever-existent." The eternal nature of the soul is manifested in its power of knowing the eternal. But the soul is not simple. Its mortal part is not the work of the supreme creator, but of the "younger gods"; and it therefore does not have the same high destiny as its loftier part. The soul that in our bodies is a temporary visitant "hath elsewhere had its setting and cometh from afar," even from the supercelestial world of the Ideas. As the Ideas are eternal, so it is eternal. Like the Ideas, it is uncreated; but, unlike them, it is not unchangeable and cannot remain in that world of pure Being; for though of all things it is nearest akin to the Ideas, it is not itself an Idea. Through its power of thought, by which it makes itself conscious to man, it can infallibly attain to a knowledge of the Ideas, the only true realities, of which sensuous phenomena are only the imperfect pictures. Upon the existence of the Ideas depends the immortality of the soul.

The fall of the soul from the transcendent sphere of Ideal Beauty and Goodness, and its consequent enforced entrance into the region of matter and Becoming, is the result, according to certain of the dialogues, not of a strictly moral transgression but of the rebellion waged by its preëxistent inferior parts, the spirited and the concupiscent, against the rational element. The "fall" is intellectual because it is due to the enfeeblement of this rational part. In a more developed stage of his teaching Plato makes the soul uniform but regards it as assuming certain temporary phases due to its implication in the body. In its proper nature it is the pure power of thought and cognition, possessed of a desire to attain to the world beyond. But it is soiled by the passions of its fleshly tabernacle — a doctrine taken over by Plato from Pythagoras, and reiterated with such splendid insistence that it has never ceased to maintain its hold on the thoughts of men.

With the death of its contaminating associate the soul departs to receive either reward or punishment in a nether purgatory. It has not ceased to retain some remembrance of its celestial abode where it had once seen Pure Beauty and Pure Truth; and if its recollection of that divine home is but little impaired, when the moment comes for it to reënter the life of the body, it will choose an existence corresponding to the nobler associations of its previous sojourn in the world of sense. If it has drunk deep of the waters of Lethe and feels only a faint stirring for the world beyond, because it has not waged war successfully against the impulses and passions of the body, it will elect a baser lot and may be reëmbodied in the form of an animal or a plant. All souls are condemned alike to the circuit through the great cosmic cycle.

Birth and death follow each other in succession. But death is not merely release from the body; for, as the late Dr. Adam has well said, palinoenesis is opportunity for evolutionary conversion; with each new stage of existence we are "assimilated to God," and grow from flesh unto spirit by the systematic exercise of reason, which effects the purgation of the soul from ignorance and the arrogance of false knowledge.

The souls of the philosophers require only three periods of reincarnation of a thousand years each, the grosser souls ten thousand years, before they can return to the place whence they came. Then at last, freed from the delusions of sense and the penitentiary punishment of reincorporation, they ascend to their true home, the realm of Pure Being, where they can again contemplate the eternal Ideas, above all the sovereign Idea, the cause and reason of all Being, the Good, which is God; and there even in that supercelestial world, where space is not, nor time, nor anything that changes, they retain (strange mystery) their conscious personality unimpaired to all eternity and are not lost in the Universe. But the souls that admit of no cure are consigned to a life of eternal misery in Tartarus to serve as awful warnings of the consequence of unhallowed deeds.

Plato is both a visionary and the first thinker to deal scientifically with the problem of immortality. He has absorbed, transformed, intellectualized the faith that had quickened the spiritual life of the sixth century. He has radically emancipated religion from nature-cult. If he has given the soul an intermediate place, in the dichotomy of mind and matter, between unchangeable, imperishable Being and fluctuating phenomena, he has attributed to it alone — in its rational aspect (for the Greek thinks spiritual things in terms of the intellect) — the power to discern the Eternal Ideas in their purity. "The thinking part of the soul elevates us from earth to our kinship in heaven, because in truth we are creatures not of earth but of heaven." Plato has kept the religious value of Orphism, for he has shown that the soul is the divine part of man and that it is the presence of this divine indweller in us that makes us truly human; for "man is most truly man when he most resembles God." The divine inhabitant in each of us is an exile from its true home; it longs with a great passion to be free from the wild desires of the senses with all their joy in deception. The beauty of this world reflects only afar off the divine Beauty of the other world; it stirs our sluggish memories; it is a challenge to regain the sight of the undeflected Beauty. Of itself the world is evil. Our heavenly nature calls inexorably to us to reject it and to flee hence with all speed. "Our flight brings us nearer to God." We are strangers here, and human things are after all not worthy of life's struggles, life's ambitions and splendors. It is by "the study of death" ($\mu\epsilon\lambda\acute{\epsilon}\tau\eta$ $\theta\alpha\nu\acute{\alpha}\tau\sigma\nu$) that we realize our immortal nature; only by the contemplation of Ideal Beauty does life really become worth the living; by our progression through various lives the thraldom of the senses loses its insistence and the power of reason is quickened in its "chase" after the eternal verities, so that at last we grow into perfect knowledge. As the immortal part of us, the soul can gain through purification, through moral asceticism, the beatific vision which is its ultimate goal. Since man in his essential nature is divine his highest purpose is to become like unto God. To pass through the gates of death is to attain to the Supreme Good.

THE END